TEACH YOURSELF TO SWIM
ELEMENTARY BACKSTROKE FOR SAFETY

A **TEACH YOURSELF TO SWIM**
e-Book Series
IN ONE MINUTE STEPS

"You can easily transfer these familiar motor skills to the shallow end of a pool or lake on a weekend or summer trip"

By

DR. PETE ANDERSEN

http://www.LearnToSwimProgram.com

http://bit.ly/FaceBook-LearnToSwimProgram

http://bit.ly/YouTube-LearnToSwimProgram

https://www.Pinterest.com/LearnToSwimProg

www.SwimVideoCoach.com

www.YouTube.com/SwimVideoCoach

www.TeachYourselfToSwim.com

Your comments and www.Amazon.com reviews are welcome.

JOIN OUR MISSION TO HELP SAVE MORE LIVES!!!

Enjoy and pass along what you learn to others

Trius Publishing, P.O. Box 600801, San Diego, CA 92160

TEACH YOURSELF TO SWIM ELEMENTARY BACKSTROKE FOR SAFETY

Copyright © 2016 by Dr. Pete Andersen
Published in the United States by:

Trius Publishing, P.O. Box 600801, San Diego, CA 92160
www.TriusPublishing.com and www.DrPeteAndersen.com

All rights reserved. No part of this e-book may be reproduced by any mechanical, photographic, or electronic process, or in the form of an audio recording nor may it be stored in a retrieval system, transmitted, or otherwise be copied for public or private use—other than for "fair use" as brief quotations embodied in articles and reviews without prior written permission of the author and publisher.

The author of this book does not dispense medical advice or prescribe the use of any technique as a form of treatment for physical or mental problems without the advice of a physician, either directly or indirectly. The intent of the author is only to offer information of a general nature to help you in your quest for performance improvement. In the event you use any of the information in this book for yourself or to help others is your constitutional right, the author and publisher assume no responsibility for your actions.

Paperback ISBN: 978-0-9899468-7-2

ASIN: B01D0FABI2

List of paperback / Kindle books and DVD sets in the

TEACH YOURSELF TO SWIM series -
IN ONE MINUTE STEPS [or Your Child] TO SWIM

ISBN # / ASIN #   Title

ISBN / ASIN	Title
978-0-9820248-7-4 B00TSV32EC	TEACH YOURSELF OR YOUR CHILD TO SWIM AT HOME WITHOUT A POOL
978-0-9820248-2-9 B00TXWW284	TEN BEST STEPS TEACHING YOURSELF TO SWIM SAFELY AND EFFICIENTLY
978-0-9820248-8-1 B01CYYTQPO	FLOATING RELAXED
978-0-9820248-9-8 B01CZK84FK	FREESTYLE WITH BREATHING
978-0-9899468-0-3 B01CZK8971	USING YOUR OWN FEEDBACK
978-0-9899468-1-0 B01CZLEH2S	USING SIX NEW TEACHING METHODS
978-0-9899468-2-7 B01CZLERQY	BACKSTROKE THE EASY WAY
978-0-9899468-3-4 B01CZM0KU0	WATER SAFETY CONCERNS IN OTHER ENVIRONMENTS
978-0-9899468-4-1 B01CZMM846	WATER SAFETY RESTING SKILLS
978-0-9899468-5-8 B01D0EO3VO	IN DEEP WATER WITHOUT FEAR
978-0-9899468-6-5 B01D0FA7S6	SHALLOW TO DEEP WATER PROGRESSION
978-0-9899468-7-2 B01D0FABI2	ELEMENTARY BACKSTROKE FOR SAFETY
978-0-9899468-8-9 B01D0FP9HU	BREASTSTROKE THE EASY WAY
978-0-9899468-9-6 B01D0G7VDY	ADVANCED WORKOUT SKILLS
978-0-9820248-3-6	Active Lifestyle (3 DVD set 5 hours 37 minutes)
978-0-9820248-4-3	Parents, Grandparents, Beginners, Non-Swimmers, Instructors (4 DVD set 7 hours 24 minutes)

978-0-9820248-5-0	Competitor Masters, Senior Olympians, Triathletes, Age-Group Swimmers (2 DVD set 3 hours 21 minutes)
TBD/ASIN	Ten Best Steps Teaching Yourself to Swim Safely and Efficiently (1 DVD 1 hour 15 minutes)

Series of single DVD disks of the same content as the e-books is being completed as of this printing. They will be available on Amazon and my shopping cart for under $10.

See fast link below.

You can order from

www.Amazon.com/Books

www.Amazon.com/Videos

OR   order directly from the website

www.LearnToSwimProgram.com

shopping cart using the fast link:

http://bit.ly/1NdevtV

Most of these are under $10 to get you started.

Author's Personal Message of Introduction

In August of 2010 I heard a news report of nine related African-American teens that drowned in the Arkansas River trying to rescue each other. My emotion immediately shifted to thinking how I would feel losing one of my six kids or now thirteen grandchildren.

I sat down in a chair and cried for about twenty minutes. And then I got mad thinking how could teenagers not even know how to make a human chain to interlock wrists to wade in and rescue someone in a current?

That thought prompted another, "How can we teach people to swim in rural and low income areas where there is no pool or an experienced instructor like to me to show them how they can teach themselves to swim?" For the past 50 plus years since I learned to teach swimming as a high school freshman and went on to earn my B.S. and M.S. teaching degrees in health and physical education at Indiana University I have monitored the evolution of swimming instruction.

At Indiana I was also a 5-time NCAA Division I All-American coached by the legend Doc Counsilman who later coached Mark Spitz and our winningest 1964 and 1976 U.S. Men's Olympic Swimming Teams and a string of six NCAA Championships.

From Doc and my teaching degrees I learned how to apply all the physics principles to learn to swim instruction. At the same time to finance my graduate degree I was a Director of Aquatics for Country Clubs and a large Chicago suburban high school and park district of 80,000 people. I directed and trained all our high school student instructors to teach swimming to our community grade school children in our Saturday morning and summer swim school programs.

Before I started in my first teaching and head coaching position I had already been teaching swimming for ten years. But after four more years gaining valuable director experience running large programs I felt I needed more knowledge.

I went back to graduate school to earn my Ph.D. in psychology of learning principles with emphasis in behavioral and educational psychology and statistical analysis. I completed a three year program in two years because I was allowed to collect dissertation data while I was attending classes.

Another reason was because my wife at the time and I had triplet boys born three months into my program to add to my three-year-old son.

Between helping at home bathe, feed, and change diapers, and going to classes and teaching classes as a grad assistant I only got an average of four hours sleep.

With my swimming pedigree the University put me in charge of teaching most of the college swimming courses. And for my dissertation I tested our 1972 U.S. Men's Olympic Swim Team and six of the top ten NCAA Division I teams.

All throughout my degreed programs it was impressed on all students to embrace professional growth - to keep learning. Over the years teaching thousands to swim and hundreds to be quality instructors I found that my students taught me!

I would change my method or cue and see how they would respond to learn that skill faster. Later now in my book and videos I have introduced six new teaching methods no other instructor or program is using.

I had already added physics principles and now added psychology of learning principles from my Ph.D. I've learned that no other instructor in the world has achieved. Coupled with having swum and been a 5-time All-American mentored by the greatest swim coach of all time I am blessed with very good skills.

Using these skills and my desire to prove my system of easy-to-master one minute steps gets faster longer-lasting results, I got back into competitive swimming with the U.S. Masters Swimming. It took six years of training to set my first World Record, and since I've always been in the top 10 in the U.S. and FINA World Rankings for my age group. I have also achieved 21 Senior Olympic Summer Games Championships Gold Medals with records to match.

I like to tell people it's not like I'm a man telling a woman how to have a baby. I practice and prove what I teach every day. My proven results and ability means I know how to correctly demonstrate and teach the correct visual, verbal, and most important kinesthetic or feeling cues with imagery techniques to speed up the learning process.

My system is now proven to get faster longer-lasting results because it follows a system of sequential steps to make it easier for the brain to learn. The imagery cues I use are universal to children and adults like floating level as an air mattress, or reaching over a barrel or a ball to get your hand catch and arm rotation correct for example.

In the summer of 2010 when those nine teens drowned I took action and sat down to write up a sequential curriculum for all the strokes. I also wanted to write in simple terms to explain how never out-of-date physics and psychology of learning principles would be applied so people could learn to teach themselves to swim with my correct pictures demonstrating the skills.

This would really help save more lives especially in rural and low income areas or when people had large families. I reasoned that 1) learning to swim is a necessity and the only sport that has the potential to save your life, and 2) water has a way of finding you when you are least prepared that can lead to panic and a tragic result.

Eventually I became an expert in drowning prevention and swimming instruction to do radio interviews all over the U.S. My book and the only complete video curriculum instructional series in the world to include all the strokes plus water safety concerns in unfamiliar places were published.

To my surprise thinking that all major swim programs would embrace my work based on physics and psychology of learning as "the new science of swimming instruction" for professional growth to upgrade swimming instruction and the universal mission to save more lives that has not happened.

All the major organizations have proved very protective and unwilling to change. Therein lays the most significant problem why unintentional drowning deaths have not declined in the last few decades.

In my analysis getting all my fairly reliable statistics from the Atlanta based Centers for Disease Control and Prevention or CDC there are still on average ten unintentional drowning deaths each day in the U.S. and many more in other countries. The most likely reason is there are no pools or experienced instructors.

There are cultural issues and myths to overcome. As reported by the CDC 70% of blacks and 60% of Hispanics do not know how to swim. The worst myth is that blacks have heavier bones and smaller lungs and cannot float. What a lie that is!

In the 1000's I've taught to swim I've only had two black males who were body builders with only 6% body fat that were negatively buoyant. But I still taught them how to swim.

If the mother does not know how to swim their child has only a 13% chance of learning how to swim. But if a child learns to swim before the age of four they have an 88% chance of surviving a water accident.

Now you can see the importance I place on teaching parents how to start teaching their babies to swim at home without a pool at 2-18 months when they bathe them. This process is no harder than teaching their kids to learn and improve any backyard sports skill to transfer to the playing field or court.

I try to change all that at home without a pool using their kitchen sink, dressing mirror, mattress, and a bathtub. Now they can get familiar with all the basic physical motor patterns at home without fear of drowning.

Then when they learn at their own pace and feel confident they can transfer those same familiar skills to the shallow end of a pool or lake where they can stand up. I even teach people how to float with their mouth open to make a better air lock with their nose and how to use goggles to see the pool bottom to place their feet and stand up!

When a lot of people live in rural areas or have large families and cannot afford pool admission or lessons my "TEACH YOURSELF TO SWIM" system helps solves this growing problem to help save more lives.

Rather than waste any more time with other swimming instructional organizations and programs I have elected to use technology and social media to reach out to people in need to save them time and money and frustration. All my content is available on Amazon, select bookstores and swim outlet stores, and my website www.LearnToSwimProgram.com or shop directly using this link http://bit.ly/1NdevtV

I've learned that kids like adults don't like to waste their time when they are not learning from young inexperienced instructors who cannot demonstrate or teach with correct methods and cues because they are not being taught how to teach by the organizations. They make certification a joke in the U.S., but not in Australia or New Zealand where I have visited and had meetings with their organization directors. You have to prove your ability to teach before they will certify you.

The result is that most of the kids taking lessons today never master their rhythmical breathing to swim continuously any distance to save their life. Even their floating skills are poor. And worse, they never learn about wave actions, currents, marine life, and hypothermia to avoid risks.

The #1 reason why people unintentionally drown is because they overestimate their swimming ability. Most learn in a clear heated pool with goggles. And once they pass a minimal test they are cleared to have fun and go off the diving boards in the deep well. So they think they are good enough swimmers because they can make it from the diving board to the ladder.

But that won't help them in an ocean rip or river current or fast moving stream in a flood. Boys and young men are the worst at getting their macho ego involved to overestimate their ability. So I created the mental skills swim test.

Sit down in a chair and close your eyes. Now imagine swimming out into a lake 100 yards where you cannot see the bottom and the water is only 70 degrees. That's only the length of a football field. Okay now rest a bit and swim back.

If you took a gasp or deeper than normal breathing cycle, or your heart rate started to increase slightly, then you are not as good a swimmer as you think you are. Kids on swim teams would have no problem doing that.

Of the ten people who unintentionally drown each day two are children generally under the age of four. But the other eight are adults! What percentage of those eight adults probably took lessons as kids? So why has the number not been declining.

Could it be that large organizations are not willing to upgrade their swimming teaching methods and cues to reflect the new science applying physics and psychology of learning principles?

That is what I am all about and have proven results so you can benefit from in the contents of my work producing a book and video curriculum series. I believe I can teach you better on your own TV or downloading my chapters to your tablet to take to the pool or lake than any young inexperienced teacher.

And now for the first time I have created a series of e-books, paperbacks, and video disks devoted to only one smaller part of the curriculum at a time to make it even more affordable for everyone to teach themselves. My system of easy-to-master one minute steps is embedded in each product's content so you can get faster longer-lasting results, save money, time, and most important improve the overall safety of your family.

After you invest and use any of my products I'd like to learn your comments. You are also going to get a series of three "fast-start" tutorials for free you can forward to all your friends and family on emails and links to the tutorials on your social media. Together we can help save more lives.

Sincerely,

Pete Andersen, Ph.D.

For free swim tips www.LearnToSwimProgram.com/Swim-Tips or use this link http://bit.ly/1NdevtV to shop

*** FREE BONUS OFFER ***

Get valuable FREE content. Forward a copy of your Amazon Kindle book receipt to: drpete@LearnToSwimProgram.com OR ... complete the easy form on my website www.LearnToSwimProgram.com/Subscribe   OR ...

Scan the code or text or voice mail your name and email to 1-858-886-9820
and
I will give you my download to my

Best Selling e-book valued at $9.97
"Teach Yourself or Your Kids to Swim
at Home Without a Pool"

AND

My popular nine page article
"Tips to Prevent Drowning"

AND

Get three valuable "Fast-Start" tutorials & podcasts

AND

Please provide your book review. Get the fast link from

http://www.LearnToSwimProgram.com/Amazon-Reviews

Find us on ...

http://bit.ly/FaceBook-LearnToSwimProgram

http://bit.ly/YouTube-LearnToSwimProgram

https://www.Pinterest.com/LearnToSwimProg

www.LinkedIn.com/In/DrPeteAndersen
www.Twitter.com/DrPeteAndersen

To give me permission to send you
VALUABLE FREE content, or
go to leave a comment or ask your question:

http://www.LearnToSwimProgram.com/Contact-Form

and submit the easy form

****

To find out how to achieve all your
swimming strokes, water safety
and more, go to:

http://www.LearnToSwimProgram.com/Resources

The following contents are listed for you to choose
your level of interest.

Would you benefit from more quality **FREE CONTENT** tips, webinars, and videos to get faster longer lasting results?

Could your Age-Group or Masters Swimming Teams benefit from a $3,000 - $7,500 easy "turn-key" program **FUNDRAISER**?

Would you like to be rewarded for recommending our quality books/DVDs to your family, relatives, friends, neighbors, co-workers, teammates, using your e-mail and social media? Then be sure to sign up for our **AFFILIATES** program? It's easy.

Would you like to continue improving your water safety knowledge and swimming skills in a monthly **GROUP MEMBERSHIP** that meets every other week, gives you more resources, and can get all your questions answered?

Do you desire All-American level **PERSONAL COACHING** to take your skills and fitness to the next level with Skype?

Would your organization, association, corporation, or team benefit from one of my professional instructional **CLINICS**?

Would you like to join our mission to save more lives by qualifying to become an **AMBASSADOR** and enjoy getting valuable discounts on books, DVDs, clinics, group membership, and personal coaching?

Imagine enjoying swimming better with family and friends. It's easy with my easy-to-master one minute steps system.

Imagine saving your money and time and getting faster longer lasting results from a pro instructor! Then if you take local lessons you'll get more out of them.

To find out how to achieve all these things and more, go to:

http://www.LearnToSwimProgram.com/Resources

TABLE OF CONTENTS

	3	List of paperback books and DVDs in series
	5	Author's Personal Message of Introduction
	11	Free bonus offer
Chapter 1	15	Change your mindset to learn more
Chapter 2	25	Need for water safety knowledge and skills
Chapter 3	32	Personal guarantee and disclaimer
Chapter 4	34	Your personal benefits teaching yourself
Chapter 5	44	What to think before you start to improve
Chapter 6	54	Floating principles
Chapter 7	57	Back float progression
Chapter 8	61	Back float to swim progression
Chapter 9	66	Elementary backstroke progression
Chapter 10	70	Elementary backstroke kick sub routines
Chapter 11	74	Elementary backstroke kicking for power
Chapter 12	77	Child guidance - breaststroke kicking in wall brace position
Chapter 13	80	Elementary backstroke kicking on back
Chapter 14	85	Elementary backstroke arm progression
Chapter 15	87	Elementary backstroke timing your arms and legs
Chapter 16	90	Water safety proof

Ch. 1 Change your mindset to learn more

There are short chapters in this e-book. There are easy-to-master steps as you progress in a number sequence that is capitalized sub titles. You now have the opportunity to learn a variety of swimming skills, and not just freestyle. Floating is an essential skill few beginners or even advanced competitive swimmers take time to master. But you should. If you think you know how to perform all these skills, guess again. Just do them in sequence to know for sure and build your confidence. Mastery is a challenge to keep learning and perfecting all your swimming skills. Take this e-book with you to the pool and learn all the steps in stages, a few or many at a time depending on your current skill level.

This illustrated book with sequence pictures is changing the marketing strategy for teaching swimming worldwide. People have been conditioned to believe they cannot teach themselves or others how to swim because they think they need a pool or body of water to learn the basic skills. My aim is to bring swimming instruction into the home or public arena where there is no pool or body of water nearby, then show you how you can easily transfer the same identical elements of the basic motor patterns learned at home to shallow water in a safer environment.

You can build basic swimming skills as motor patterns in the brain in your own home using a kitchen sink, dressing mirror, bed, and bathtub as easily as learning to play and catch balls in your back yard. With your help my social media marketing approach will reach more people and save more lives.

There are several reasons why ten people drown each day in the United States. The biggest reason is that under the current marketing system, you have to live in metropolitan areas with pools to find instructional programs. And then you are not assured of an excellent curriculum, experienced instructors, and teaching methods and cues that get faster results. People living in rural areas or low socio economic status suffer graver consequences.

If you were not provided with instruction when you were a child, it's hard to find an adult class. Young and inexperienced instructors do not feel comfortable teaching adults because they can't think like an adult. They worry about having to make a save or performing mouth-to-mouth if an adult should happen to suffer a heart attack from over exertion caused by swimming inefficiently, and not floating very well.

You know your children should learn how to be safe around water when you go on vacations, but realize an average private swim lesson will cost you $20 per half hour or is marketed as a book of five lessons for $100. Instead of taking the time to master the basics at home to get more out of those lessons, you watch a young instructor beg your four-year-old to put his face in the water for the first 15 minutes. Cha-ching ten bucks! Forget that you have 2, 3, or 4 other children who also need lessons.

Maybe $100 is not a problem for you, but this amount poses a serious problem worldwide for low income families who can't afford even the pool admission. But those parents want to protect their children, too. I want to help more people easily learn how with better skills for as little cost as possible.

This e-book introduces new methods of swimming instruction based on the science of physics and psychology of learning principles. My marketing plan is to get this book and video series interpreted into as many foreign languages as possible. I will make the program available through foreign government distribution to their masses to save more lives. Social media, affiliates, and joint venture partners will also play a critical role to reach more people worldwide.

This is not a franchise that has a limited market based on profit with little quality control. There is no costly recurring franchise, pool membership, or lesson fees that can be as high as $1,000's of dollars. Everyone who invests in this book for under $20 and/or adds the videos for a package of $97 can continue to review and share in this resource with your family and friends. Perhaps you could encourage your local library to make this investment, and your whole community or school system can check it out and reach more people.

Water provides a fun playground and can also be very unforgiving. It only takes a few minutes to drown. There are many communities that do not have pools, quality instructors, or a curriculum to follow. There are few adult swim classes to improve your skills.

As a pro with expert credentials and experience I can assure you quality instruction to learn how to swim correctly the first time, and not have to unlearn bad habits that create your inefficient and exhausting movements. **You have the ability to teach yourself many skills, but you have to take action. You cannot learn what you do not start.** Home hardware and improvement stores depend on your ability to view, read, and follow their simple step-by-step directions to learn how and complete projects. In school you had to read the book and take notes to learn new information, process it, and take action.

If you can play catch with your kids, you can teach them basic swimming skills at home to start without a pool. Videos and pictures in a sequence along with specific how to instructions using visual, verbal, and kinesthetic feeling cues easily teach you how. The sequential system and mastery of each step along with four other teaching methods are my keys to getting fast results.

National and local swim programs generally do not spend time teaching water safety concerns outside of a clear, heated pool. When you overestimate your swimming and floating ability, you get fooled in unfamiliar water environments. You get caught in undertows, rip currents, or river currents, and do not use caution around marine life because you do not know what to do.

Many adults, despite having learned how to swim in an instructional program, never master how to do their breathing to swim continuously without building up an oxygen debt and stopping in the pool. You may be one who swims inefficiently with your head out of water the whole time to quickly exhaust your muscles and breathing. Floating skills are essential when you cannot stand up on the bottom and need to rest.

Learning to swim with your breathing efficiently helps you maintain your active lifestyle longer. When you learn to float you can swim better, and increase your effort to improve your cardio-vascular fitness.

The national problem is that 60% of adults cannot swim 20 feet to save their life. You either never learned how to swim or swim so poorly you fear not making it in the deep end of the pool trying to do fitness laps.

Fear of drowning is a terrible phobia. Overprotective parents can unknowingly condition this behavior, and unless you break the cycle you could be instilling the same fears in your children!

Fear robs you of all the potential water borne recreation you could be enjoying with your family and friends. <u>YOU</u> could be having more fun, too, by taking action to learn how to teach yourself now with all the simple easy-to-master steps in this book. You will learn all about hypothermia, wave action, currents, floating and physics principles, propulsion, resistance, and the psychology of how we learn skills. You have the opportunity to learn how to swim several different strokes and resting skills if you get into trouble, and be more confident in and around water.

This week, by chance, I spoke with Doug who said he had just turned 40 but did not know how to swim. His kids knew how, but he would sit in the boat while they had fun in the water. This is more common than you may know.

Several years ago on a hot night I went to swim laps at the park district pool in Apple Valley, MN, but had to give up because they had not set up lap lanes. As I stood at the wall in the pool next to a middle-aged couple, their son swam in and out like a fish. She said to her husband, "I wish I could swim like that."

I knew then why I was directed to the pool that night. I put my goggles up on my forehead and politely told her I was a swim pro, and could teach her how. In 20 minutes she was able to swim 15 feet out to her husband. In another 20 minutes we worked on the pool side to show her simple drills she could use to teach herself how to condition rhythmical breathing to swim continuously non-stop.

The point of these two stories is all about readiness. You can safely walk across the street to get to the other side when you look both ways. When you take that action, you increase your confidence with the knowledge YOU put in your brain that it was safe to cross.

Learning to swim is a lot like that. **YOU have to take action to decide to learn.** That is your first step. When you accomplish the first step, this leads to the next simple step in a progressive sequence of steps you can master because **YOU CAN DO** each step. Each step rewards you enough to want to continue learning more and more until you become more confident and skilled. This is why my illustrated book has over 300 mini steps using my 6 unique teaching methods and specific cues that are different from any other program to teach you how to teach yourself.

The rules are simple. YOU cannot advance to the next step until you master that step. If you think you already know how to swim, then it should be no problem for you to start with step one and do each perfectly! In no time you will be where you think you wanted to be when you started in my program. If you violate this rule, then be prepared to hold yourself accountable when you are not satisfied with your performance.

I do not recommend you start on any higher step than #1. Your brain needs to be conditioned or retooled to do these fundamental motor patterns correctly. There is a reason why my sequence of steps works!

YOU may find a missing link in your knowledge and skills that will improve your performance when other strategies and tips you have tried in the past have not worked well. If you choose to start on a higher step, and find you cannot do that step very well you must agree to drop down to the previous step or steps until you can prove to yourself that you can do those steps well. Keep stepping back until you find your weak link that causes you to be inefficient.

My first week of practice at Indiana University, my coach, Doc Counsilman (who became the World's Greatest Swimming Coach), directed all of us including our All-American's and World Record Holders to do push offs and glides, and dives off the blocks for distance.

Back in 1961 Doc was a fat guy, but he could dive in off the block and on one breath glide the whole lap or 75'. I don't know what the other guys were thinking, but I thought, "Wow. If this fat guy can do this, I can, too!" I don't think I made it halfway on my first few attempts, but I did keep improving until I could make it about 65 feet.

The point of this is that you learn the most about laminar flow from your skin and other sense organs to reduce resistance when you are barely moving. You learn how to stretch and streamline your body to reduce drag resistance. Depending on the length of your race and your physical conditioning, you lose great amounts of time when you become tired and create more resistance perhaps the last 10% of your race.

Conditioning through workouts can help you acquire the optimum pace to conserve energy, and not degrade speed at the end of your race. But if you never took time to learn how to use the water and the physics of buoyancy and laminar flow, none of this will matter. If this practice to learn such a fundamental skill was good for Doc and World Record Holders, why do you think you are any different?

This illustrated book and optional hours of step-by-step instructional videos explain how to overcome your fears and relax so you can float in a variety of ways. I have six unique teaching methods no other instructor uses to communicate clear, concise messages you can process and physically perform. I also take time to explain numerous water safety concerns so that once you learn how to swim and get out of the pool into another environment you will know what to expect and be prepared.

An ounce of prevention is still worth a pound of cure especially when a human life is involved.

You will also learn basic physics principles like Newton's Three Laws of Motion, Bernoulli's Principle, and the psychology of learning to condition new motor behaviors to make them permanent. Then I will show you how to apply your knowledge to swimming correctly and efficiently to conserve your energy by being able to process your own feedback wearing goggles.

Swimming efficiency is simply based on reducing resistance to the body moving through water while increasing the surface area and force involved with propulsion over a longer range of motion.

I frequently refer to **DPS or distance per stroke. It is far better to take a few good strokes than a lot of fast poor ones** and go nowhere while expending 10 times the energy to use up your oxygen and get into trouble.

If you or someone you know look like you are climbing out of the water, you are not using the physics force of buoyancy to assist you. Have you ever observed a beach ball full of air skimming over the water in a slight breeze? Don't even think of going after it or an air mattress or inner tube. Let someone in a power boat go retrieve it. When swimming, always keep a reserve supply of air to inflate your lungs at all times.

Children grossly overestimate their swimming ability and easily get into trouble outside of a pool environment. They also regularly tell their parents they know how to swim, and their parents believe them!

I know how to paint, but I am not Van Gogh or Picasso. Swimming skills have this same variability. Just because you can swim 10-20 feet does not make you a good safe swimmer in different environments.

All park district pools have lifeguards that make kids and adults pass a swim test to go into the deep end. That test is usually 50 yards or two lengths in a 25 yard pool. What or how kids swim that test only matters if they can make it without stopping. Unless they are on a swim team, 99% of them swim with their head completely out of the water switching back and forth to breath.

How long could you last swimming so inefficiently 2, 5, or 10 minutes? If YOU swim like that because you never learned how to swim with your breathing, YOU have a problem.

Whether it is <u>YOU</u> or your children or your grandchildren, you must be sure of your swimming skills to be efficient. **IT IS NOT GOOD ENOUGH SIMPLY TO SAY YOU ALREADY KNOW HOW TO SWIM.**

The true test of your swimming ability is to take a walk in the park - only you will use the pool to swim some distance <u>NON-STOP</u>. If you can relax and float, take long slow strokes, exhale in the water 20% of your air like you do when walking, and inhale 20% back in to supply enough oxygen to your working muscles to keep going, then you will have passed the critical test.

The problem is that many instructors want you to start swimming right away. They breeze through the floating skills you still need to master to relax and not tense up. They unconsciously create the mindset that if you don't rapidly move your arms and legs you will sink.

Stiff muscles use up your oxygen quickly. To get more oxygen you lift up your head, but this drops your hips and legs down. Now you're swimming like a barge instead of skimming like a water ski. This inefficiency creates more demand for air to quickly exhaust you and put you in trouble.

Another great problem is that as a parent you falsely assume that if your child is taking swim lessons he will learn how to swim and be safe. You probably give more thought to choosing your dentist, and certainly would like to know if your surgeon is board certified and performed more than a few surgeries successfully.

You probably also assume that the instructional methods and curriculum are sound because they are the Red Cross or YMCA - huge national programs. But this does not mean the instructors have been taught how to teach correctly by experienced swimming professional teachers like me using advanced teaching methods and cues. My guess is that less than 1% of all instructors have even heard of Bernoulli's Principle and how to apply this principle to their swimming instruction.

The problem with some national and local programs is that they are out-of-date because they have not changed their standardized teaching methods or cues to get better predictable results. There is no quality control. High school aged kids make up the bulk of the summer instructor group, and they are lucky if they have already had physics to apply those principles in their teaching.

Requiring a standard to pass on to another level in a program is a good idea. But to require all the instructors to teach the same outdated methods and cues is like asking a college professor to teach the same way for 20-30 years, and how would that benefit those students?

Large or small franchised programs provide no guarantee of experienced instructors. In fact, many instructors have only been teaching for a few years or months, and are not competitive swimmers to know kinesthetic "feeling" cues from advanced personal skills they can demonstrate. How can you provide the correct cue to learn if you have never felt the result?

When I taught my high school instructors who would teach our local grade school children, I would not allow them to wear long-sleeved sweatshirts on the deck. You cannot demonstrate the visual arm position to develop the correct motor pattern if you cover up the arm. It is how the brain learns, but instructors violate this every day.

To summarize:

1. Don't overestimate your swimming ability.
2. Tell your kids, "Don't tell me you know how until you can show me all the basic skills."

3. Choose your swim program and instructor(s) wisely to know their credentials and experience.
4. Ask to see their curriculum or teaching lesson plans.
5. Be able to pass the "Walk in the park" test.

About Teaching Yourself

Home improvement companies like Home Depot, Lowe's, and Menard's have done well marketing the idea that with the right tools and instructions you can make simple and some complex repairs or construct things for your home. Their "how-to" guides take you through a sequence of steps. This is like the swing set instructions you used to put that together. Each step is so simple it only involves placing nut B on bolt A.

When you went to school, your teacher created verbal images, showed examples, demonstrated some skills to give you a visual idea of what to copy, and then verbally provided specific instructions how to perform parts or segments in a sequence. In some cases you took notes to recall how to do the sequence of events. Other times, you had to immediately translate what you were told - all the cues - into a physical action.

What I do is the same only instead of a teacher providing immediate feedback about how close you came to correctly performing that skill step, I teach you how to judge your own feedback. You will use goggles, your ears, eyes, and feeling receptors in your hands and forearms and other body parts to feel the water pressure and assess your movement efficiency.

If you are an adult who never learned how to be relaxed and efficient, it's hard to find an adult swim class. This book and video package fills that gap. You may also live in a part of the country that does not have pools - indoor or outdoor. You may have to use a back yard above ground pool, you cannot push off the side or swim more than 10-15 feet, but you can learn a lot.

I have lived in parts of the US where the "swimmin' hole" was a deeper part of the local creek. Rivers, lakes, and oceans can be dangerous places to learn because they have swift currents and wave action. The water is not as clear as a pool to provide good feedback on how you should be performing the skills underwater as shown in the videos and book picture sequence. With any coordination your brain can process the information like when you were in school to teach yourself to swim like a pro.

You can't finish learning how until you start to take action. Follow the steps and practice them all until mastery and you will be pleased with your results.

I find that many people have the mindset that if they don't move their arms and legs they will sink. They also think that if they rapidly move their hands and arms through the water that they are swimming better!

Efficient swimming is based on two simple principles: 1) You want to float and **decrease resistance** to your forward progress created by any body part outside an imaginary midline or plane cutting through your body like a spindle or rod to roll about on that axis, and 2) **Increase propulsion** of the surface area and lengthen the range of motion of that force application.

Imagine a water ski rope stretched out underneath you. As you take a freestyle stroke you reach out in front of you in the midline plane and grab hold of the rope. Then you pull yourself forward the first half, and push yourself forward the second half of each stroke to move over the top of the water.

If your body is not moving forward with little effort because you are floating, then you are not using proper mechanics to hold on to the water. **You have to learn to feel the water pressure on your hand and forearm with each stroke** as if you were reaching over a barrel. If your hand and arm are slipping by, then you are like a car spinning your wheels on ice.

> **It is far better to take a few good long strokes than to take a lot of short fast poor ones.**

Ch. 2   Need for water safety knowledge and skills

1. DROWNING STATISTICS

The Centers for Disease Control and Prevention in Atlanta Georgia report credible statistics each year. As stated before, ten people drown each day in the United States. For children ages 1 to 4 drowning is the leading cause of death. Children gain easy access to plastic, inflatable, and above ground backyard pools that are not fenced in. By race, African-Americans and Hispanics experience a much higher unintentional drowning rate than Caucasians.

Males account for 80% of unintentional drowning victims. The statistic that struck me the most was that children 14 and younger grossly overestimate their swimming ability, and unintentional drowning is the second leading cause of death in this group. This means you cannot assume your children know how when they tell you they know how to swim. Get them to demonstrate their swimming and water safety skills and compare that skill against a known standard that you have observed from pictures in this book or the videos available on my website: www.LearnToSwimProgram.com/Swim-Tips.

Kids get familiar with swimming in their local clear heated pool. Most swimming programs do not teach more than pool safety concerns to learn what to avoid or do in other aquatic environments. This leads to serious problems when parents or grandparents take them on vacations to the ocean, large lakes, fast-moving streams, and on boating excursions.

Knowledge and understanding the forces of water in wave action, currents, undertows, and hypothermia prevent panic and unintentional drowning. However, few swimming instructional programs take the time to explain what can be expected in other aquatic environments. Every grade school and high school, with or without a pool, needs one physical education class period set aside in the curriculum to learn about other aquatic environments.

Many parents use lifeguards as kid-sitters while they relax and don't watch their kids. You must assume personal responsibility for your swimming safety, and that of your immediate family and friends. While lifeguard training has improved immensely over the last 10 years, there are elements that lifeguards have no control over that can cause drowning such as stepping off piers or swimming in unmarked areas with breakwaters, rocks, wave action, currents, etc.

There are common factors that create accidents in and on the water. The most obvious is the use of alcohol while operating a boat, jet-ski, or other motorized equipment. In 9 out of 10 boating accidents the person who drowned was not wearing a life preserver. For every drowning there are four near drowning victims. In many of those cases the brain is deprived of oxygen that can cause serious brain injury for the rest of one's life.

When your children say they know how to swim, do not assume they can swim any kind of distance or have floating skills that enable them to be relaxed and comfortable to rest in other kinds of water environments.

Many of the teaching methods and cues in swimming have not changed or been modified much in the last 50 years.

Children have an 88% higher chance of surviving an aquatic accident when they know how to swim. There is no other sport you can learn that has the potential to save your life.

I would like to think that all of the national and local swimming instructional programs provide a good basis for efficient swimming for the rest of your life. But until all programs are fully capable of teaching you how to master all the necessary skills to be efficient for the rest of your life, take the time to master each step to become totally proficient.

2. KIDS OVERESTIMATE THEIR SWIMMING ABILITY

As was previously reported by the Centers for Disease Control in Atlanta, children 14 and under grossly overestimate their swimming ability. Once a child feels like he can swim a short distance to qualify to swim in the deep end and go off the diving boards, he feels safe. At that young age they have energy to burn, but that does not mean they have mastered the fine art of swimming efficiently. Consequently, when they grow up to be adults and want to swim out to the raft, they may think of themselves as still being 12 years old, but they are still unskilled and easily get into trouble without knowing resting skills to recover well enough to save their own lives.

As a parent or grandparent, you want to make sure that all your children can demonstrate efficient swimming skills for a variety of strokes for a variety of situations that can be expected when they leave the swimming pool. Once you have observed their proficient skills, ask them to start teaching their friends those skills. Challenge each and every one to continue learning to be efficient in the water.

3. UNDERSTANDING PANIC

When you are not familiar with what to expect and are unskilled to control a life threatening situation, you can easily go into panic mode. In a state of panic your brain literally shuts down its thinking capacity and subconsciously shifts toward self-preservation. You are not conditioned to know that you should take a large breath and hold it in until you float to the top. Then you can level off with less resistance to swim to safety.

What typically happens when people are tossed into the water either out of a boat or off a pier, they begin to struggle immediately because they do not put their heads and chests down which would raise their legs and hips up. Victims exhale but do not inhale to inflate their lungs to float. When they arch their heads up above water to breathe, their hips and legs go down vertically preventing forward swimming.

Panic victims will reflexively exhale their air as their diaphragm breathing muscle tenses up. Then they pant like a dog, but do not forcefully inhale enough to inflate their lungs to help them float. They quickly become exhausted and sink.

One of the critical steps that I condition is to take an immediate breath and hold it until your body floats to the surface keeping your head down to raise up your hips and legs. Once you are leveled off you can begin swimming to safety with less effort.

In cold water, parkas and heavy outer wraps absorb water to weigh you down like a wet sponge. You must wear a life preserver to stay afloat. If your lungs do not displace enough water to buoy you up like a balloon, you become a dead weight and sink after your muscles become rigid and exhausted from all the adrenaline. This only takes a few minutes.

Always remember that, **"An ounce of prevention is worth a pound of cure."**

The best prevention is learning how to swim efficiently with more skills, knowledge, and understanding of other environments besides your local heated pool.

Change your mindset from feeling like you have to rapidly move your arms and legs or you will sink. Instead, think about fully inflating your lungs and floating on top of the water. Then level off to use your arms to pull and push your body on top of the water with a mild kick to keep your legs up. Floating is key to your efficient success in swimming, and you will spend time learning to improve your floating skills.

With floating skills you can swim in almost any kind of environment with the knowledge that you will not sink and can go with the flow wherever that water takes you in a wave, stream, or a current of any kind.

4. LEARNING HOW TO IMPROVE YOUR SKILLS

The easiest way to determine if you are improving is if you are moving when you take strokes in the water. If you are taking lots of strokes and not moving, you would have to assume that you are not stroking correctly and are inefficient. This is your personal feedback.

I teach you first response conditioning to take a breath and hold it until you can level off and start stroking. Once you are floating, it takes little or no effort to pull your body over the water unless you are vertical or perpendicular to the water surface. Then you will expend lots of your energy and air and go nowhere but down.

By learning in small segments, you will feel rewarded and motivated to continue learning that next new step having mastered the one before it. Your job is to feel more consciously aware of your improvement. You can do this by pushing off and gliding across the pool for a set distance, and try to improve upon that distance each time you do a push off. The idea is to float relaxed and swim effortlessly across the pool.

The thumbnail photographs provide a standard to judge how well you are performing each of the steps. When you're able to more closely copy the sequence pictures in the book you should feel success, and transfer the same identical elements to the pool starting in the shallow end to eventually swim in the deep end with the same skills.

5. THE RESPONSIBILITY FOR YOUR PERSONAL SAFETY IS NOT YOUR LIFEGUARD'S

A swimming pool or beach may post lifeguards, but this does not relieve you of your personal responsibility to practice safe swimming. You must practice your skills to feel comfortable in the environment you are going to swim.

Cold water can bring on hypothermia faster than you might think. It can take your breath away, and cause your muscles to rapidly tighten up and lead to exhaustion in a few minutes. In water less than 50 degrees you may have less than an hour before you pass out and drown. In colder climes, it's wise to check the weather report and the boat you might board before you venture on to cold water. That fish is not worth your life.

6. YOU ARE NEVER TOO OLD OR TOO YOUNG TO LEARN HOW TO BE SAFE FOR FITNESS AND RECREATION

Swimming is a learnable skill for almost everyone. However, you must have an open mind to process the cues, and have the flexibility in your muscles and joints to perform the proper movements. Efficient swimming does require some flexibility. But you can also make several adaptations to decrease resistance and increase propulsion just as well.

Swimming is a great fitness activity because water has more resistance than air and reduces the effect of gravity on your joints. But if you fear not being able to make it to the deep end, you may not prefer swimming to maintain your cardiovascular fitness. My aim is to teach you efficient techniques you can easily learn and apply now so that you can maintain your active lifestyle in to your 80's. When you master these skills, teach others to join you in workouts, and join the US Masters Swimming organization www.USMS.org to gain valuable coaching tips, and promote "Swimming Saves Lives" on their website.

For recreation, water has endless possibilities. Besides boating you have lap swimming, water skiing, inner tubing, rafting, sailing, kayaking, canoeing, fishing, surfing, body-surfing, windsurfing, snorkeling, SCUBA diving, skurfing, and kite boarding to name a few various types of water recreation. I have done almost all of these. These kinds of activities are what keep you young and fit for many years to come.

A great resource is www.NDPA.org - The National Drowning Prevention Alliance. On their website you can find tips to prevent drowning, safety awareness campaigns, and a list of quality swimming schools. To get your child involved in competitive swimming go to www.USASwimming.org to find a local team.

Go to http://www.USSwimSchools.org to locate a quality swim school in your area.

You can email me: drpete@LearnToSwimProgram.com with questions or use www.LearnToSwimProgram.com/Contact-Form

You can get my current address and office telephone number from my website:

www.LearnToSwimProgram.com

You can subscribe, friend, or leave a comment, like or share suggestions for improvement

http://bit.ly/FaceBook-LearnToSwimProgram

http://bit.ly/YouTube-LearnToSwimProgram

https://www.linkedin.com/in/drpeteandersen

http://www.Twitter.com/drpeteandersen

For continuous improvement and coaching help, enroll today in my monthly Q&A Blue Ribbon Group program on my website.

http://www.LearnToSwimProgram.com/Membership

Normally it's $27 and valued over $150 in lessons!

Here's what you get each month:

1. Two 50-60 minute instructional/coaching webinars followed by your questions you can ask ahead of time so if you cannot attend, you'll hear your answers on the replays

2. Each week a new Chapter video from the curriculum in sequence to cover all the strokes plus water safety.

BONUS DISCOUNT

For getting my book(s) and becoming a part of my family of friends and Ambassadors of Swimming, I reward you with a lower enrollment fee of only $17 per month.

YOU MUST USE THIS DISCOUNT CODE AT CHECKOUT

SWIMFAST

Ch. 3   Personal guarantee and disclaimer

7.   MY PERSONAL GUARANTEE AND DISCLAIMER

If you follow my prescribed sequence of steps and practice enough to master each step, you will learn how to swim. For the videos you have 30 days unconditional guarantee from the date of shipment. If you are not committed to learning and practicing, then I would prefer you defer your investment or gift someone in need.

This guarantee is null and void if you are physically and mentally unable to read and/or perform any or several of the skills due to obesity, joint flexibility, injury, deformity, muscle weakness, sprains or strains, or mental condition.

I am not a medical doctor prescribing medical advice. I have a Ph.D. in how we learn motor skills based on psychological principles. From my personal experience, I may explain how I avoid swimmer's ear and fungus infections simply by drying out the outer ear canal with toilet paper on my little finger. This personal practice is not dispensing medical advice.

What you choose to take from this book is at your own direction. What knowledge and skills you choose to share with other people is your right, and I encourage you to help save more lives.

8.   THANK YOU FOR TAKING ACTION

It's never too late to improve your lifelong swimming skills. It's easy to believe that unintentional drowning and near drowning happens to the other person. But if you watch the news, you probably have learned about someone in your area who has drowned in the last two years.

I want you to be completely satisfied with the content of this book and/or the videos. You can search on Amazon and find that there is no instructional swimming video series available. There are competitive coaching technique videos which is entirely different from my instructional series.

This book benefits the active lifestyle, parent and grandparent, competitive Masters, Senior Olympians, and triathletes as well as the non-swimmer or novice and inefficient. Instructors benefit by learning new teaching methods and cues that get fast results and save more lives.

You purchased this book to improve your swimming efficiency. You will need to continue to take action to learn each and every step in the sequence for this to be effective for you. As you master each small step you will feel a sense of accomplishment and be motivated and challenged to learn more in the next step. Build your support network by telling your family and friends what you know and are doing.

I have coached All-Americans and know that coaches like to tweak the fine points, but sometimes neglect the imbedded fundamental motor patterns that cause the confusion and prevent improvement in efficient technique to swim farther and faster. Not all great coaches are also great teachers. The psychology of learning in my six teaching methods plays a greater role than the simple application of physics principles.

Use your feeling of reward to build your confidence and motivation to learn all that you can from each of these steps. Being able to say that you know how to swim is not enough. You must also be able to say with clarity that you are comfortable swimming other strokes and in all kinds of aquatic environments by knowing the action and force of water.

Ch. 4   Your personal benefits teaching yourself

9. VALUE COMPARISON TO TEN ½ HOUR PRIVATE LESSONS AT $30 PER ½ HOUR

If you were to take ten ½ hour private lessons from a swimming instructor, he would charge you a minimum of $20-30 per ½ hour. This would include time spent for him to explain and demonstrate a specific skill, and your time practicing to master that skill. At the end of your 5 hours of instruction, you would probably know how to swim one stroke - freestyle, but perhaps not yet with efficient breathing technique.

Otherwise, why do so many adults and kids (except those on swim teams) still swim with their heads out of water at the local pools? You may be exposed to other strokes such as backstroke, breaststroke, and elementary backstroke, but not have time to master them without additional lessons. You may have never been taught excellent floating and resting skills to apply in open water when in trouble. But I will teach you these fundamental safety skills now if you will only take action to learn them.

A parent with two kids or more has to keep paying for multiple lessons for all the kids when one investment can provide all the fundamentals you will need for all of them as well as your friends and other relatives.

I also take time to teach you the equivalent of at least one lesson on water safety concerns outside of a clear heated swimming pool. In my experience, I have found that many instructors do not get in the water, and are not able to demonstrate the skills as they should. You will see a sequence of thumbnail pictures demonstrating how to do each skill. I've not found many instructors who spend time teaching you about water safety concerns outside of the pool. One result is that people get into trouble in unfamiliar environments on vacation.

Along with the visual picture sequence you'll be given a detailed verbal explanation of how to perform each skill that includes kinesthetic or feeling cues. These cues in combination prove highly resistant to forgetting and condition you to master each skill faster.

For a small investment, this paperback book provides a lifelong resource benefit you can take to the pool to review and compare to your skills. You also have the opportunity to invest in several hours of a complete DVD video instructional curriculum of easy-to-master steps. Ordinary lessons require repetitive payments. You have to decide their value based on results for a return on your investment. Good experienced instructors do make a difference, but there are not enough of them in all parts of the world.

In lessons, most of your time is spent listening to your instructor explain what I show you how to teach yourself with personal feedback cues. The video series provides a resource that you can continually refer to and share with all of your family and friends, and maybe split the investment to learn at your own pace and not feel rushed to get your money's worth.

As your body composition ages losing strength and flexibility, or if you suffer from a temporary injury or setback, sometimes those lessons you took several months ago are forgotten. But with the videos and the sequence pictures in the book, you can review, learn, and practice your skills on your own time.

10. WHY AND HOW _YOU_ CAN TEACH YOURSELF THE RIGHT WAY

The benefit of illustrated pages is like putting together a swing set in your backyard. Manufacturers provide you with a visual step-by-step sequence for you to put the swing set together with just a few basic tools. You must read the pages, follow the specific instructions in sequence, and then apply and process that information until you get it right.

Read the pages and steps in this book to follow the step-by-step sequence. You may mistakenly think that you can do any of these skills and skip around them. Well, prove it to yourself that you can. It will only take you a minute if you already know how. **The sequence is the key to mastery.** Each small step that you master in that skill makes it easier to learn, reward, and master the next step and so on to continue learning more advanced skills.

If you are not learning to improve today, it is because you stopped learning before mastery of key steps like coordinated breathing to swim freestyle continuously.

If you are a competitive swimmer and not getting any faster, you may not have mastered the spatial awareness to provide good body position and streamlining to reduce resistance.

I assume that you can process visual, verbal, and kinesthetic cues and have enough joint flexibility to perform each fundamental skill. If you are physically unable to perform a specific skill, you will need to make an adjustment to your stroke so that you can still perform that skill reasonably well. Your focus will still be on floating, streamlining, and propulsion.

I take complex skills and break them down into several sub routines or smaller parts that you can easily master with a little practice. Then I chain the sub routines together to perform the entire actual skill. This is why you must follow the specific sequence that I suggest for you to learn faster and be able to teach others.

11. VISUAL DEMONSTATIONS, FEELING CUES, VERBAL HOW-TO DO INSTRUCTIONS

The thumbnail sequence pictures show you how to perform what you are reading about feeling cues. More complex skills will have a set of sub skills or sub routines to learn in smaller steps. When you practice these sub skills in the water or wherever they may be such as at home in front of the dressing mirror or on your bed, pay close attention to the feeling cues that I suggest for you as well. Visualize your body and its position. Talk to yourself and self-correct if you are not in the position that is described in the words and pictures.

The human mind has a great ability to copy what it sees. Visualize in short term memory, and copy those skills by telling your body parts what to do. This is my teaching method known as mind control over your body parts.

This is not rocket science. When you were a child, you were able to toss a ball up into the air and catch it. Swimming is as simple as that. You get a general idea, and then once you go to the pool in the shallow end you perform exactly as you had imagined or visualized that skill in your mind.

12. FEEDBACK CUES TO SELF-CORRECT YOUR PERFORMANCE

My instructions give you specific feedback cues to help you self-correct your performance. Wearing goggles helps to see what you do underwater.

Several of these cues require you to focus on what you are feeling when your hands and arms are entering the water. For example, if you don't feel water pressure on your hand and forearm when you begin to pull in the freestyle you are probably not pulling correctly. With your goggles you can see if you are reaching over a barrel or dropping your elbows to let your hand slip through the water after it enters.

Think of a car spinning its wheels on ice. The wheels turn very fast but the car does not move forward. Moving your arms and legs rapidly can be like that. You get the impression that you are swimming when you are not.

You float first and swim second. <u>Feel the water pressure on your hands and forearms to pull and push your body forward.</u> Look at the bottom to see if you are moving forward. It's better to conserve your energy and air supply by taking a few good strokes than a lot of fast poor ones.

Wearing goggles allows you to observe your swimming strokes above and below the water. In some steps you'll be standing in waist deep water to see your arm pattern as it performs each skill. You will condition the feeling in your hands and arms with what you see yourself doing compared to my demonstration. You can learn self-correction skills and not feel dependent on someone to tell you.

13. LIFETIME REFERENCE TOOL, NEVER OUT OF DATE

When you learn to teach yourself, it's easy to teach others and I hope you do to save more lives. The skills I teach you are more than what you might find in other books and programs at this time. The skills you master now will be as important 20 or 30 years from now for you, your children, and your grandchildren to master equally as well.

Using easy-to-master smaller sequential steps you can learn more swimming skills that many hours of private lessons do not provide. To be comfortable and skilled in the water you need to swim other strokes besides freestyle. To do a survival float or tread water, you must have floating skills and kick breaststroke. If you get into trouble and need to rest, you should know how to roll over on your back and float to recover your breath. This means you need to know backstroke floating and swimming skills, and sculling.

I see adults on vacation and nearly all of them swim with their heads and faces out of the water. They never learned to master their breathing as children in their swim program. Inefficient swimming leads to quick exhaustion that gets you in trouble, but this book illustrates how you can learn to teach yourself to master your breathing sequence and swim continuously like a walk in the park.

14. SHARE THE TOTAL CONTENT SEQUENCE WITH YOUR FAMILY AND FRIENDS

My hope is that when you learn to swim efficiently you will recall all of these specific cues, strategies, and teaching methods to teach others around you. This goes beyond your immediate family to your extended family and friends. My mission is to save lives. I need your help to learn these skills correctly and teach them to others. If you feel uncomfortable doing that then please offer to share the book (or videos) with others or recommend how they can invest in their own personal copy.

Knowledge of the forces of water and what to expect helps you avoid danger. Share your knowledge to keep others safe, too.

15. BONUS FEATURES – SAFETY AWARENESS, MORE ACTIVE LIFESTYLE

I spend a considerable amount of time educating you about other water safety concerns. However, this information will do you no good if you do not take the time to read these chapters. Water is everywhere. It's estimated that 65% of all recreation involves water.

If you live and play in and around water you must master these basic skills. Most of the awareness skills I will teach you are common sense. But you cannot assume that your children or your grandchildren have your common sense. Otherwise, for children ages 1 to 4 the leading cause of death would not be drowning.

My personal concern is that children 14 and under grossly overestimate their swimming ability. This can easily get them into trouble outside of a swimming pool. You may live next to the ocean, but this does not mean you are safety aware and efficient in your swimming technique. I have spoken to many people who live next to the ocean, and they are no more skilled than a person growing up in rural Kansas.

Parents, you cannot assume your children are as skilled as they think they are. You must have them frequently demonstrate their skills to you. Once they can demonstrate all of the skills in this book, you'll be more reasonably assured of their ability to protect themselves in and around the water.

I cover oceans, lakes, rivers, streams, and ponds to explain wave action, currents, marine life and hypothermia. I will also explain how to avoid electrical storms and electrocution, use proper equipment, and understand weights and measures to respect the power of moving water.

16. EASY TO UNDERSTAND CUES, IMPROVE EFFICIENCY, AND FITNESS

A cue is a stimulus to trigger a conditioned response. Over the years I have found that the cues used by several national programs are no longer effective to aid learning some skills. It is difficult for some of those national programs to change their curricula. This is a gross error of cause and effect. If you keep doing the same things and get the same poor results, then you must change what you do to get better results.

I provide you with specific cues that get fast results using my six unique teaching methods. You only have to focus on one body part at a time. My 50+ years with proven practical experience as a college All-American, coach of All-Americans, Masters World Record holder to correctly demonstrate these skills, and a doctorate in how we best learn motor skills, I have found that these cues work the best.

I use spatial awareness as the first of my six unique teaching methods to get you to focus on only one specific body part at a time, and know where that body part is in space. Take, for example, the pattern movement of your hand in and out of the water. If your mind is processing other kinds of sensory information, this will not help you to learn. I immobilize other body parts like having you stand still on the bottom of the pool for your brain to focus on only one arm or grasp the wall with both hands to blow large bubbles.

Once you build the specific motor pattern, you can transfer that habit to a pool much easier than if you were to try to couple that particular skill with other specific parts all at the same time. To your benefit, this is the value of my sequential system of steps. You get to learn at your own pace.

When you feel yourself in the water going farther faster with less effort, you become aware of your improvement to self-reward your skills in one-minute steps to keep you motivated. It is easy for you to monitor your performance. When you take a stroke, if your body is not moving forward for the amount of effort you have applied, you get immediate feedback that you may not be doing that skill efficiently. I teach you how to process your own feedback to learn self-correction skills so you can teach yourself to swim like a pro.

I provide you with an accurate visualization and verbal explanation with feeling cues to copy and compare to your performance. When you see accurate and effective movement for the amount of propulsion effort you apply, you feel rewarded and want to continue to learn more. This is why I use 300+ steps in my sequence so that you will feel frequently rewarded in one minute steps.

17. KNOW WHAT TO LOOK FOR IN AN INSTRUCTOR AND PROGRAM

As with any service whether you employ a contractor to lay tile in your home or build a deck the final outcome is called results. You can ask for references from people who have taken lessons from a private instructor to determine his effectiveness. You can ask for a copy of the curriculum to learn what you are paying for in what time frames. You can ask who the instructors are, how they are trained, and their experience. You can gauge this by their ages and whether or not they can perform the skills they are asking their pupils to perform.

Do not be fooled by the fact that a program provides certification. Paramedics never ask whether a drowning or near drowning victim was ever certified. It is hard to enforce quality control for any instructional system. This book and videos provide some basis to compare swimming instruction. If those "certified" cues are out-of-date, they are always out-of-date. Can the graduates swim with their breathing and know other strokes and survival skills?

Typically there are student instructors who are also lifeguards at your local pools. Hopefully, they are or have been on a swim team to accurately demonstrate and verbalize skills. But it's not likely that inexperienced student instructors will understand how to apply all the physics and psychology of learning principles found in my six teaching methods and numerous cues that get results until they read my book.

You can be assured that if your instructors get in the water they are more likely to be able to perform the skills they are asking their pupils to learn. Because a learner copies visual patterns it is imperative that the instructors do not wear bulky clothing such as sweatshirts, jackets, and sweatpants. The student will not be able to visualize the discrete curvature of the arm, the positioning of the legs in the kick, and the application of propulsion in the demonstration if the teacher is wearing bulky clothing.

As a rule, instructors will not produce a written curriculum with educational objectives, a detailed sequence of specific steps, or spend time teaching mastery of floating skills and all the water safety concerns for other environments as I do.

Many programs do not motivate their pupils to continue to learn more and more skills. Unfortunately, once parents and kids feel that they can swim a short distance, they think they are safe when they really are not. To be safe in and around water you must be able to swim continuously some distance and not just enough to swim in the deep end by passing that short 25 or 50 yard swimming test. It upsets me to see lifeguards pass students in this test who swim the entire distance with their head out of water never mastering their breathing technique.

These children grow up to be adults who make common mistakes going out to the raft thinking they can swim like they were 12 years old again. They may not master one of the most basic resting skills to simply roll over from your stomach to your back and float to recover your air because you've spent all of your energy in your poor efficient technique.

You may tend to think that you are safe because you can swim a short distance or have a life preserver handy, but the drowning statistics kept by the Centers for Disease Control in Atlanta, GA report that for 9 out of 10 boating deaths due to drowning, the individuals were not wearing a life preserver.

18. DON'T TELL ME; SHOW ME

The biggest mistake you can make is to assume that you know a skill before you perform that skill. Don't let your kids tell you or let you tell yourself that you know how to do something until you can actually do it. If you are that skilled, you can do each step in about one minute. If you find a step is too difficult you may need to go back to the previous step in the sequence, and spend more time to master that step and several of the steps prior to that one.

As you become more familiar with specific skills or tasks, your proficiency will gradually increase to help you learn the next step more easily. The value of taking the time to practice and master each step makes you feel rewarded for your accomplishments.

19. SEE CONSISTENT IMPROVEMENT AND CONFIDENCE; FEEL REWARDED

The strategy behind teaching you one-minute steps is the pleasure you feel when you master something and feel rewarded. With a very complex task like learning how to swim breaststroke you can easily be frustrated and give up. I break down this complex skill into several sub routines you can easily master one-at-a-time in a sequence I will chain together later. This process builds your confidence as you feel rewarded and motivated gaining mastery of that small step to keep learning.

It's a common psychological principle that you will want to repeat steps or skills when you feel rewarded, and avoid those when you feel failure. This is why I have broken down efficient swimming into multiple steps that you can take one at a time to improve your performance, and learn more than simply how to swim freestyle with your breathing.

After you learn how to swim freestyle efficiently, you will be challenged to learn other water safety skills and strokes to feel comfortable in other aquatic environments. I continue teaching more floating and resting skills, and then start with regular backstroke, floating, and resting skills followed by elementary backstroke, breaststroke, and water safety concerns.

All these skills together help you improve your confidence to enjoy other water activities, and maintain an active lifestyle for the rest of your life. Thus, the value is not in learning how to swim 25 or 50 yards, but in being able to swim other strokes and understand the action of water and its forces so that you are better prepared to avoid problems in and around water.

20. HOW TO USE EQUIPMENT – GOGGLES, KICKBOARD, ETC.

A good fitting pair of goggles with a silicone seal around your eyes is one of the most valuable pieces of swimming equipment you can buy. There are a number of online swim stores where you can purchase these kinds of goggles. What I recommend are the Speedo hydro-specs that you can buy from www.Kiefer.com or www.AllAmericanSwim.com.

Goggles let you see your stroke above and below the water so that you can master self-correcting skills as you compare my demonstration to your performance.

Many pools have kickboards but may not let you use theirs. They cost $8-$10 and kids jump, sit, or throw them around to break them. You can buy your own, put your name on it, and take it with you to the pool. Owning a kickboard provides you with upper body flotation to extend your arms and master the sequence and rhythm of kicking freestyle or breaststroke.

Hold the front or sides of your kickboard with your hands. Depending on how long your arms are, rest your elbows on the lower corners. You eliminate extra sensory information coming into your brain by stabilizing the board and extending your arms. You have enough room to place your face in the water between your arms and practice blowing big bubbles while you maintain a steady kick.

Ch. 5   What to think before you start to improve

21. YOU CAN TEACH YOURSELF TO SWIM LIKE A PRO IN ONE-MINUTE STEPS

There are many places in the U.S. and world where you cannot find pools or highly trained swimming instructors. Even in populated places, there are few older experienced professionals to trust learning the right methods and cues to get faster, longer-lasting results that have the potential to save your life.

Few programs spend time teaching you water safety concerns outside of your clear heated swimming pool. Many do not openly market their programs or encourage patrons whom they see not swimming well to take lessons. Learning to swim continuously with your breathing is a sure way to improve your safety and family.

If you exclude adults who were once on a swim team, my estimate is that 90% of all adults have never mastered their breathing skills, despite taking lessons as children. The consequence is that they do not prefer to swim to maintain their active lifestyle and cardio vascular health benefits.

My marketing plan is to use social media to teach you how to swim at home without a pool. You can start to learn all the basic motor skills using a kitchen sink or wash basin, dressing mirror, mattress, and a bath tub. Then you can more easily transfer these identical skills to the shallow end of a pool. If you decide to take lessons, you'll get more value out of them. I envision elementary teachers teaching all of these home skills during physical education to help save more lives.

My illustrated book and videos are a constant resource. You will learn valuable feedback methods and cues to make self-corrections to all your swimming skills, and continue to learn and improve. The benefit is that if you are injured or cannot swim indoors during the winter months for a period of time, you can use these resources to regain your skills.

The oldest psychology of learning principle is that we want to repeat pleasure (our success) and avoid pain (our failure). I have broken down complex skills into simple easy-to-master steps in a curriculum sequence to increase your probability for success every step of the way. When you feel self-rewarded for learning a step, you are also encouraged to learn the next step with confidence.

When you pay for a private lesson, half of your time is spent learning from your instructor how to do a specific skill. Too often, your instructor may not get in the water to properly demonstrate that skill to get a visual idea as well as my photo sequence shows you. You pay for your performance/practice time. Whether you read my book and view the photo sequence or videos using methods and cues based on my 50+ years of teaching experience to know which get results, or listen to your instructor's explanation, you still have to process the information which is teaching yourself.

If your children take lessons, your charges multiply quickly when you could have taught these basics at home first. This is no different than teaching your children baseball, soccer, basketball, or golf skills they transfer to the game.

22. SHARE YOUR SUCCESSES WITH OTHERS

My book and video series is based on physics and psychology of learning principles. You benefit in getting the best methods and cues I have tested over 50 years of teaching which give you the best results and a constant valued resource to share with your family, relatives, friends, co-workers, and neighbors.

Do you want to get faster longer-lasting results learning to swim? Go to http://bit.ly/FaceBook-LearnToSwimProgram and subscribe to http://bit.ly/YouTube-LearnToSwimProgram

Learn about my six unique teaching methods, sequential steps, and numerous cues before you sign up for lessons. To get useful swim and safety tips plus how to choose a swimming instructor and program go to my websites www.LearnToSwimProgram.com & www.SwimVideoCoach.com

As each new swim season approaches, use your videos to review your personal skills, and water safety concerns outside of the pool where you may vacation with your family. For example, if you are planning to go to an ocean beach, review how to identify rip currents to avoid them.

You also get to learn at your own pace. You don't have to feel rushed because the hour meter is ticking off dollars in your private lesson. I teach you self-correction skills to gain valuable feedback observing your stroke mechanics above and below water using your goggles. Your body composition changes with aging or you can be injured to get out of swimming, and will need to correct some errors to remain efficient.

An instructor can only give you feedback about what you are performing at that moment in time and how to correct that specific mechanical error. YOU must still process that information and make the correction. Your instructor cannot do this for you. When you pass on what you have and know, you help save more lives. I am truly grateful for that.

23. YOU DID ALL THE WORK AND YOU GET ALL THE CREDIT

This is the 1200 seat two pool facility dedicated in 1957 where I learned how to teach swimming over 50 years ago. In March 2011, it was officially renamed the William Dobson Burton Aquatic Center at Evanston Township High School, Evanston Illinois to honor my coach. Dobbie passed away five months after the rededication of the pool, but what he taught us about life through competitive swimming lives on. My swimming instructor's instructor was our Director of Aquatics, John Terhune, who has long since passed away. Our progressive station system and curricula skills were copied by many high school programs at the time.

I will never forget riding home on the bus in late April my freshman year after teaching Saturday morning classes to our local grade school kids. We had to be assistants our first year. In our sophomore year after we proved our teaching skills, we could be primary instructors. On this Saturday morning, the primary instructor did not show up, and Mr. Terhune asked me if I was OK to take the whole class, and I did.

Going home on the bus I reviewed my morning and recalled a little boy who did what I instructed him to do. He swam (soloed) for the first time. Boy, I was hooked! From then on, I wanted to be a teacher and swimming coach because of my early experience with these two fine men.

Later, I would become close to two more fine men: Doc Counsilman and Hobie Billingsley the swimming and diving coaches at Indiana. Doc has passed away. This past July, I went over to Bloomington, Indiana to help all the divers celebrate Hobie's 85th birthday. And what a great motivational speaker he is today! I still get goose bumps listening to his stories about personal challenge.

The nice thing about swimming is that you have no one to blame for your lack of success if you learn to "pay the price" as coach would say. Later, I would recall this as a major paradigm shift in my life. **Quality of effort equates to quality of reward.**

YOU have to take action. I believe that if you have applied the sequence of steps and taken the time to master each one, you'll have quality results to show for your quality effort. Only you can judge the worth of your personal effort.

All I know is to keep trying to improve at whatever I choose to do. **In life I have viewed myself as an average person who tries to do a better than average job.** These skills and knowledge take time to master. There are no shortcuts to excellence.

The turtle was a plodder who beat the faster rabbit. Your values and priorities may be different. But **I can assure you that if you value being an efficient swimmer, you will also want to teach your children and friends what you know to pass on what I have taught you.**

My mission is to save lives while improving the quality of life through swimming activities. I want to thank you for whatever steps you have taken to help yourself and others.

You deserve all the credit.

24. YOUR CONFIDENCE IN THE WATER IS MUCH IMPROVED

Never take for granted any small accomplishment you achieve! You will feel a sense of accomplishment by achieving any small step. You feel rewarded, and this enhances your intrinsic motivation to keep improving to maintain the good feeling you have. This builds your confidence in the water. The more knowledge and understanding of the powerful forces of water to be efficient in swollen streams, currents, and waves, the more your overall safety awareness increases.

25. DON'T LET YOUR CHILDREN TELL YOU THEY CAN; HAVE THEM SHOW YOU WHAT THEY CAN DO!

Children and adults all the time tell me they already know how to swim. Then when I see them swim with their heads out of water the whole time, I understand why drowning is the second leading cause of death for children 14 and under. It's not a good idea for parents and grandparents to think that their children are safe at guarded pools, and beaches. Lifeguards have to watch over many people at the same time. This is a tedious job. Lifeguards are trained to recognize when a swimmer is getting into trouble, but they are not your kid-sitter. In a near drowning, there is often irreversible brain damage that can require care and expense for the rest of a life.

The best prevention is to learn to swim, and know about other aquatic environments. I said this earlier. **Learning to swim is the only sports skill that has the potential to save your life.**

It usually takes a minimum of five hours of lessons to learn how to do efficient freestyle with correct breathing. This book is written with illustrations for children five and older to understand and copy what they see and read to do. The video series offers more hours of instruction that includes swimming freestyle efficiently with breathing, elementary backstroke, regular backstroke, breaststroke, resting skills, and over 20 minutes of water safety concerns.

The water is fun, and it can also be unforgiving. When I teach lessons, I don't like to play games. I want you to acquire a respect for water because it is everywhere. You cannot survive without water, but it only takes a few minutes to suffocate you. You can learn to enjoy it and not fear it. Let the water work to float and relax you. Do not fight it; you cannot win against the power and weight of water.

If you or your kids cannot easily demonstrate a specific step, then you/they must go back to master the step before it. When you stay in the sequence it makes learning the next step much easier.

26. IT PAYS TO BE EFFICIENT - REDUCE RESISTANCE AND INCREASE PROPULSION; FLOATING IS THE KEY

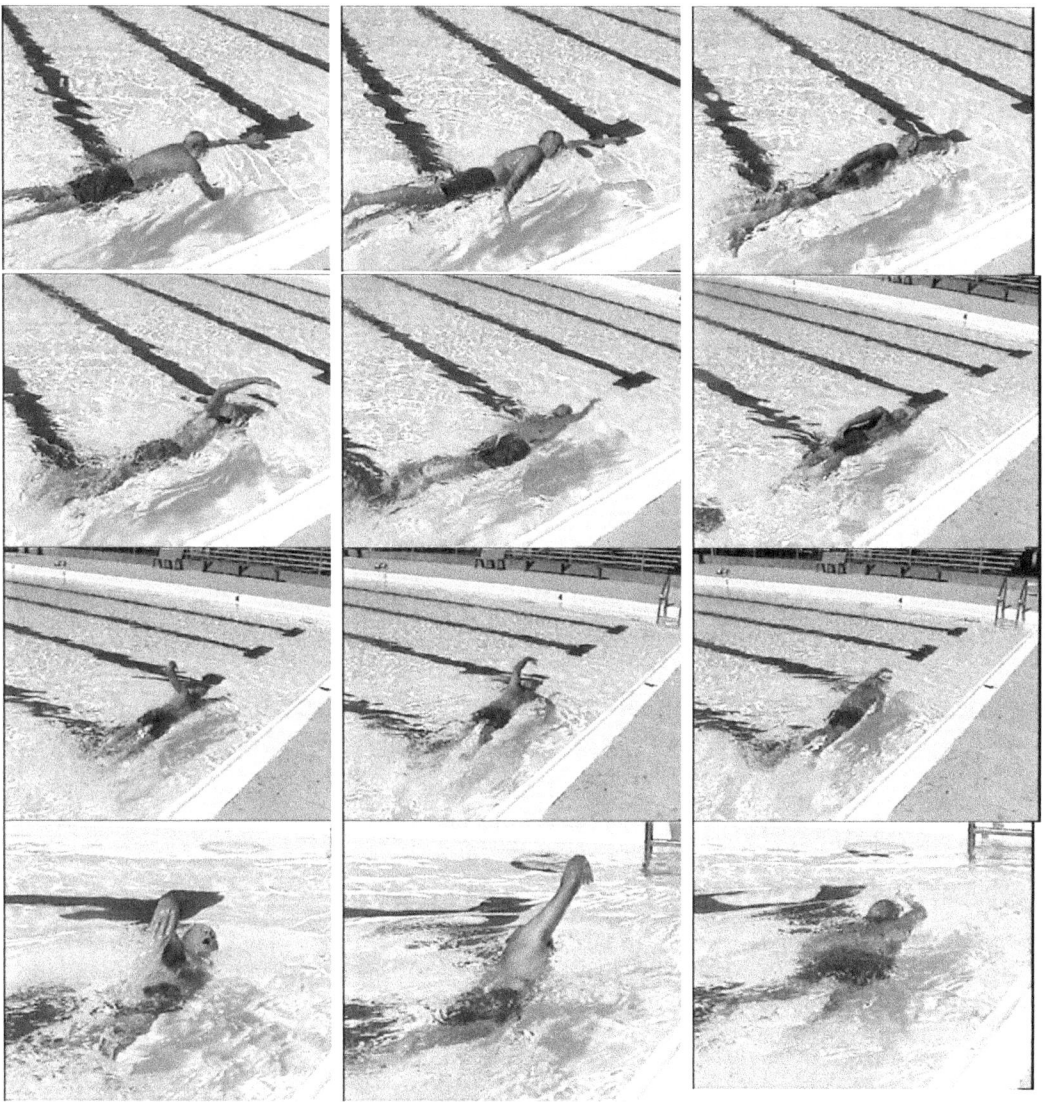

When you sign up and pay money for lessons, instructors and pupils want to try to speed up the learning process to demonstrate benefits and value. They do not spend enough time mastering the basics of floating, and move right into kicking and stroking. Students acquire the mindset that if they don't move their arms and legs fast enough they will sink.

Time is money. Once you feel you can swim a short distance, you feel safe enough to quit taking lessons and save your money. You may think you will acquire more swimming skills naturally just by swimming. However, if you've not mastered all the skills such as breathing in your freestyle to feel comfortable and confident, you can easily panic in unfamiliar aquatic situations. This is why I spend a lot of time on water safety concerns to teach you in advance what to expect so you can avoid getting into trouble.

With my six unique teaching methods, you acquire a greater understanding of how and why you must swim a certain way. I don't make the rules. There are principles of physics and psychology that tell us why we have to perform specific skills one way over another, and how we can learn them easily with good cues that get faster results.

As you age, you lose strength and flexibility. It is imperative that you reduce resistance, and acquire floating principles you may not have mastered. Once you are floating and streamlined, it is much easier to apply propulsion to move you through the water efficiently. To be competitive, all you have to do is reduce resistance, and apply more force over a shorter period of time. When the race is over you get to rest. However, out in open water you are not racing, but you may be trying to survive by conserving your energy. Now it is imperative you know how to be efficient.

Once you learn efficient swimming principles, you can apply them to any situation to save your life, swim for fun, swim for conditioning and fitness, or to compete. And, you have an illustrated book as a resource to teach you how anytime you want.

27. WHEN YOU FIGHT THE WATER YOU LOSE EVERY TIME

In an earlier lesson, I pointed out that one cubic foot of water weighs 62.5 pounds, and contains 7.5 gallons each weighing 8.3 pounds. That 5 gallon bucket of water weighs 42 pounds. Thus, a small wave can weigh thousands of tons. A fast-moving stream could have a flow of hundreds of cubic feet per minute. Whether in a flood, knocked over by a wave into an undertow, or caught in a rip current that accounts for over 80% of beach rescues coming off the beach through that sandbar, you cannot fight the water and win.

Decide right now how floating correctly will help you to go with the flow perhaps sculling on your back with your feet forward to protect your body, and slowly sculling or swimming out of the main flow to safety.

Decide right now that you will learn more skills to feel more comfortable in the water. **By taking action now, the life you save may be your own.** Certainly by learning how to apply what you learn in these steps, you can help others as well.

28. DON'T ASSUME, BE IN CHARGE, PLAN AHEAD, AND PASS IT ON TO SAVE MORE LIVES

Don't ever assume you are safe 100% of the time. It's our human error to not improve our swimming skills and knowledge of the powerful forces of water. If you go out on someone else's boat, do your <u>own</u> inspection to know the engine is in good working order, the radio and antennae work, the fire extinguisher is charged, enough gas is in the tank to get out and back, the weather report is okay, and there are enough life preservers for everyone.

You can't be afraid to say something to your friends or family. Keeping silent about a water safety concern can prove dangerous. Whether your children like to hear your lectures or not, you have an obligation to maintain their safety by any means. Whenever I see an inefficient swimmer, I stop what I'm doing and offer my help. I missed a practice just this morning helping a 62 year old woman. People are always willing to learn how to improve their skills if what you say makes sense and gets results! In 20 minutes I had her swimming when at first she would not even put her face in the water.

When you pass on your knowledge, you provide a tremendous service to help save more lives. As a resource, this content can be shared by family, relatives, and friends for a long time. Parents who have multiple children can benefit by only having to make one investment, and teaching their own children all the fundamentals they need. Swimming is a natural process that anyone can learn, if he or she is willing to try and follow my sequence.

My mission is to save more lives worldwide with good instruction to teach you how to teach yourself efficiently with good results. People in rural and impoverished urban and suburban areas without pools and/or affordable quality instruction need help, too.

You can help me in two ways by joining my mission: 1) you can invest in this book and videos and teach others what you know and have learned, or gift them a copy and 2) become an affiliate to tell all your friends, family, and co-workers, and receive good commissions for recommending the content to others so they will also invest and help save more lives. Sign up for our affiliate program by going to:

www.LearnToSwimProgram.com/Affiliates

29. TAKE ALL THE POSITIVE ACTION STEPS TO LEARN AND PASS IT ON

The life you save may be your own. It's the dumb things in life that will kill you. Swimming skills without knowledge is dangerous because it breeds overconfidence.

An ounce of prevention is worth a pound of cure. Knowing what to expect and taking proper action is key to your survival. Children, mostly boys, 14 and under grossly overestimate their swimming ability, and get into trouble in water outside of a clear heated pool. Toddlers, ages 1-4, need to wear an approved life vest in and around water. The statistics show that they can improve their chances for survival from unintentional drowning by 88% if they are taught how to swim.

Small, portable backyard pools are not fenced in. Are your kids and grandkids safe or do you just assume they are because they take lessons? And don't forget hot tubs.

As adults we forget that we are not kids anymore. Heck, I can't catch a softball over my head like Willie Mays anymore. I have not practiced that skill for over 30 years! Is swimming like that for you? What do you really know about your kid's swimming skills? Maybe they should show you all the skills in the book and videos instead of telling you they can swim. If you find they are very inefficient and have no knowledge of currents or wave action, they may be a statistic waiting to happen.

Be in charge of your life, to warn those you love, and even complete strangers. Take the water seriously. It only takes a few minutes without air to pass out. Last time I checked, humans cannot breathe underwater without SCUBA gear because we don't have gills. Totally enclose your backyard pool or hot tub to secure entry from the house, too.

Teach your family how to swim using these videos as a group activity. You teach them about life and other things to be safer. Swimming skills are no different. When you follow my sequence you can quickly build their confidence to keep learning to master the next new skill. Or, would you rather they play video games?

Are several hours of viewing my swim videos worth your time when they may save your life or a loved one like a toddler? Instead of working on your tan this summer lying out next to the pool, get in the swim with your children, and learn to improve your skills. You'll have something to show for your summer.

Use your knowledge to pass on what you know to your children and grandchildren and friends. Hardly a day goes by that I do not take time out of a personal workout to help improve another person's swimming skills. **Word of mouth is a powerful tool unless you remain silent. Then you'll regret you did not take action. At the end of the day ask yourself, "Are you improving? If not, why not?"**

Ch. 6 Floating principles

30. HOW ARCHIMEDES' PRINCIPLE WORKS FOR YOU

Archimedes demonstrated that you are buoyed up by a force equal to the amount of the weight of the water you displace. Thus, when you inflate your lungs you displace more water to provide a greater force to help you float. Fat tissue also weighs less than muscle tissue to displace more water to help you float. However, fat cannot contract like muscle to be a propulsive force.

31. NEWTON'S THIRD LAW OF MOTION - ACTION-REACTION

Newton's Third Law states that for every action there is an equal and opposite reaction. While floating, if your head weighs 16 pounds and is above the water line, then 16 pounds of force must go down below your belly button or center of gravity. This means your legs and hips will drop down if you lift your head and shoulders up out of the water. This is highly inefficient because you are technically not floating and allowing Archimedes' principle to work for you.

Your head controls your body position.

Take the time to observe how most adults swim. Many did not master their breathing as students and now swim with their head out of water all of the time. This proves highly exhausting and can get you into trouble in a hurry. This book and video series teach you how to easily master your breathing skills to be more efficient. I want you to enjoy an active lifestyle and maintain a secure environment.

32. BERNOULLI'S PRINCIPLE – BODY LIFT AND PROPULSION

 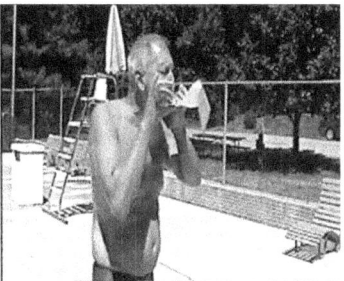 

Bernoulli's Principle states that when there is a constriction to a stream of air or water, the speed of flow will increase. If you make your body position face float look like an airplane wing, water molecules take longer to go over the top of your body and are constricted. Other water molecules speed up to fill the gap underneath you and give you slight lift. Your arm position in the freestyle pull works the same way when you feel water pressure on your hand and forearm.

When you perform your face float in the neutral position with your arms and legs fully extended, focus on trying to suck your stomach in a little so that you bend over or slightly pike at your waist. This will cause your body to look like an airplane wing, and get a certain amount of lift to keep you on top of the water efficiently. Once you start to belly out or bend backward at the waist, your head and shoulders typically rise up and your hips go down to create excessive amounts of drag or resistance to become highly inefficient.

In succeeding steps I explain how Bernoulli's principle is applied to your freestyle arm stroke and your breaststroke kick to give you maximum propulsive force. I don't believe many swimming instructors have heard of Bernoulli or how to apply this very important physics principle I learned from Doc Counsilman.

33. MORE DISTANCE PER STROKE OR DPS

When you take longer strokes while floating, you have more time to exhale and inhale and swim continuously replacing your air supply as you use it up. If you take short choppy strokes, you burn up your air supply faster, and you do not allow enough time to replace your air. This will cause you to create an oxygen debt, and you'll have to stop swimming at some point which can cause you to get into trouble with a depleted air supply.

The DPS or distance per stroke concept is how you can swim farther and faster, and use up the least amount of energy. This book and companion video series teach you how to be efficient for recreational, fitness, and competitive swimming.

If you work out to improve your cardiovascular conditioning, then apply more force to expend more effort in shorter distances and allow more time to rest in between repeats. Your oxygen debt will increase accordingly, and your body will adapt to that level of conditioning.

As you get older you lose muscle tissue and flexibility, and you have to learn to reduce resistance and increase your range of motion to improve your efficiency. If you are a competitor, the key is to maintain your body position with the proper pace. If your stroke falls apart at the end of your race, you lose.

Ch. 7   Back float progression

34. CORNER WALL BACK FLOAT

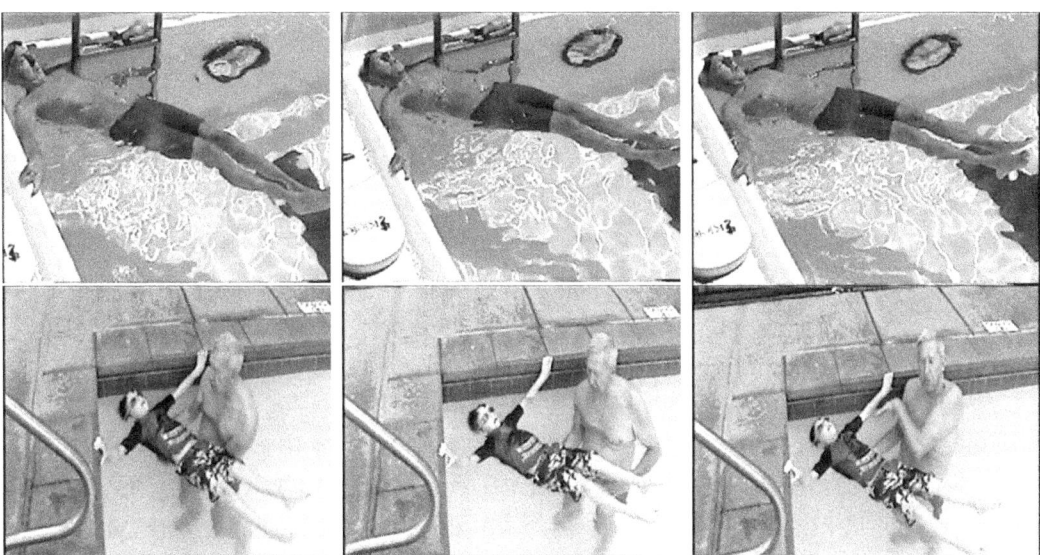

Sometimes a ladder will be in your way. Use your hands to exert mild downward pressure on top of the gutter or wall. Raise your hips and lower the back of your head into the corner until you feel your ears are wet. Inflate your lungs and feel your chest rise. You know where the wall is for your safety and security, and there is plenty of room to place your head and learn your correct body position. Bring your shoulder blades back together, and try to exert less downward pressure with each hand on the wall.

You may have to do an occasional kick to lift your legs and feet up into the back float position until you master this skill. Your head and retracted shoulder blades must be down for your hips and legs to come up.

35. CORNER WALL BACK FLOAT AND ADD A MODERATE BUCKET KICK

Start out doing your back float in a corner of the pool. Add a moderate bucket kick counting 1-2-1-2 rhythm. Depress your hands down on the wall to assist holding your hips up so they do not sink, and watch your kick. Focus on keeping your legs together relaxing your ankles going up and down to chip the surface with your big toe. The upward motion of your relaxed ankle will flipper your foot downward.

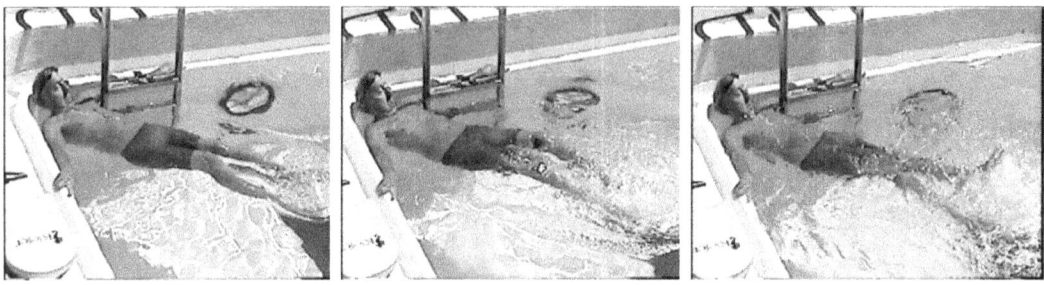

36. BACK FLOAT ON THE STEPS OR PLACE YOUR FEET ON THE LADDER, OVERFLOW WALL OR GUTTER

Place your heels on concrete steps into the pool or the ladder step that is a few inches under the water to float on your back with your arms at your sides. This will keep your legs up in a level body position so you can focus on inflating your lungs to float your upper body. This improves your spatial awareness while on your back.

Retract your shoulder blades together while lowering the back of your head until your ears are wet. Do not throw your head back or water will easily go up your nose and be unpleasant.

37. BACK TO FRONT REVERSE TO A STANDUP POSITION OR RETURN TO THE WALL DOING FREESTYLE

This bonus step demonstrates spatial awareness in your swimming ability. Start out doing a back glide perhaps adding a moderate kick, then sit down hard moving your head and shoulders forward to quickly rotate your body in a ball with your legs tucked under you. Then stretch out into a face float position. Now you can start swimming freestyle to where you started, or you can stand up in the pool. Learn to exhale slightly out your nose as your face comes forward to keep water from going up your nose.

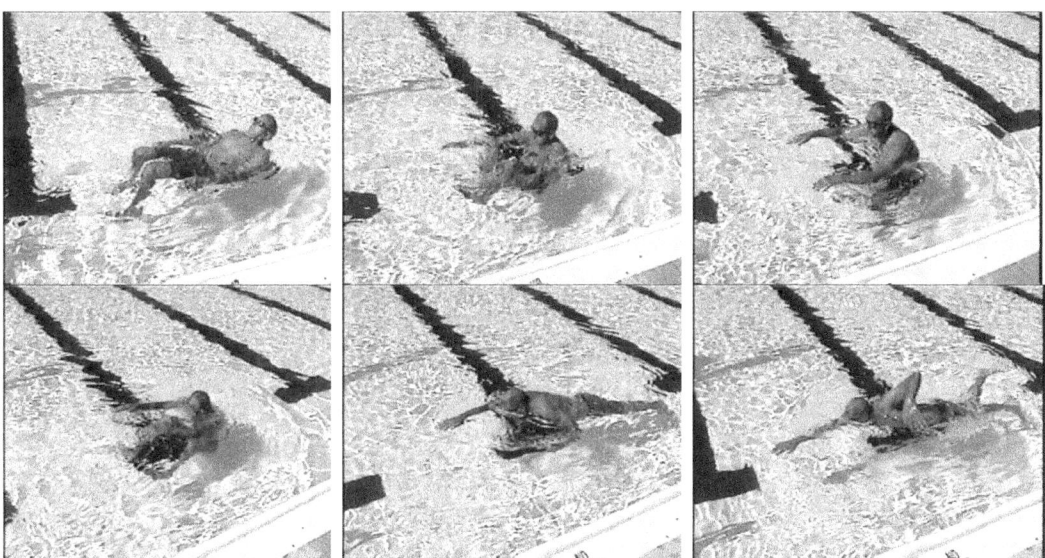

38. SAFETY CONCERN – SEEING THE NEAR OR FAR WALL CORNER FIRST

Prevent knocking yourself out hitting the wall with your head while swimming backstroke. As your arm strokes over, roll more to one side or the other, and look to the **far wall corner**. This will give you an angle to indicate where the wall is behind you. The far corner is easier to see. In some pools there may be backstroke pennant flags overhead, and you can count three or four strokes after the flags to stop before hitting the wall.

Ch. 8   Back float to swim progression - the same progressions as your freestyle sequence

39. BACK FLOAT IN THE NEUTRAL POSITION

In the back to front reverse step you did a glide first. Focus on your back float body position to be streamlined with your arms at your sides. Your shoulder blades are retracted together, and the back of your head and ears are in the water. Do not throw your head back so that water comes over your forehead to run up your nose.

As in the face float position, if your head is out of the water, your hips will go down. The same is true in your back glide and floating. Inflate your lungs to help you float, and do a moderate kick to keep your legs up. Picture your body rotating around that imaginary rod to maintain your streamlined body position. Avoid sitting down and instead force your hips up by bringing your shoulders back.

40. BACK FLOAT GLIDE INTO YOUR STANDUP POSITION

    With your hands holding onto the wall, place the ball of one of your feet on the wall. Check to see that the coast is clear to avoid blindly pushing off into someone and getting hurt. Lower your body so the water covers the tops of your shoulders. Slowly release your grasp of the wall, and mildly push off the wall with your foot keeping your shoulders level with the water surface. As you push off focus on raising your hips up into the float position, and bringing your shoulder blades together. Look back to see your feet come up together instead of throwing your head back.

    As your body starts to level off, focus on bringing your shoulder blades back together, your hips up, and placing your head back so that only your ears are in the water. This will prevent water from going up your nose. As in the freestyle, keep your mouth open to form a better airlock in your nose. At the end of your glide, sit down hard tucking your head and bringing your legs up to rotate under you. Exhale some air out your nose as your upper body goes forward to stand up.

41. CHILD GUIDANCE - HEAD CRADLE AND LOWER BACK SUPPORT

    As a parent you can make a groove with your upper arm and chest to cradle your child's head. You can use that same arm to give him slight support under his back to assist his back float. Walk backwards in the pool so he can feel the water flowing over his body. Have him do a moderate kick, raise his hips, keep his legs together, and bring his upper body and head back a little more which you can do by lowering your cradle deeper in the water. This gives him a feeling of movement in the water to gain valuable feedback about his body position.

42. REPEAT THE PREVIOUS STEP ADDING A MODERATE BUCKET KICK

In the head cradle position you can give instructions and have him observe his moderate bucket kick and count the 1-2-1-2 rhythm. He should focus on keeping his legs together and moving only his ankles up and down in rhythm. The ankle should be relaxed to kick the water up like a flipper.

43. HOW TO DO SCULLING MOTION FOR LIFT SUPPORT

Start out by squatting down in the water and filling your lungs with air to gain some flotation. Stand on the pool bottom with your knees bent like shock absorbers. Skim the palms of both hands back and forth over the top of the water. Feel the constant water pressure under your palms rotating about your wrists like small figure 8's or spreading sand out on a tabletop. The water pressure should be strong enough to lift up your body slightly while keeping your feet on the pool bottom.

44. PUSH OFF THE WALL, DO YOUR BACK GLIDE WITH SCULLING ASSIST

To avoid injury, always check to see there is no one behind you before you do your back glide. Moderately push off the wall into your back glide with your arms at your sides, and start to scull the palms of your hands. Feel the pressure, and direct in any direction you choose to go. Try going forward and backward while keeping your back float position.

45. PUSH OFF THE WALL, BACK GLIDE, AND SCULL 10-20 FEET

This tests your sculling mastery to keep your streamlined body position, and feel the water pressure to move your body. Rotate your hand about your wrist rapidly to scull. Knowing how to scull is excellent for your water safety to help you float and rest while swimming. By sculling to assist your floating, you can tilt your head slightly out of the water so you can see what your body parts are doing in your backstroke or breaststroke kicking.

46. PUSH OFF THE WALL AND BACK GLIDE FOR DISTANCE MAINTAINING YOUR BODY POSITION

As in the freestyle push off and glide to check for an efficient body position, see how far you can do your back glide with your arms at your sides. Always check behind you before you push off. Banging heads with another person hurts.

Try a two foot push off to gain a little more power. Focus on bringing your shoulders back together and your hips up to prevent your legs from sinking and creating too much resistance. Keep practicing to master this skill to improve your backstroke.

47. PUSH OFF THE BOTTOM AND BACK GLIDE TO THE WALL WITH ONE ARM EXTENDED ABOVE YOUR HEAD

Increase your practice time by pushing off the bottom back to the wall in your glide. To prevent hitting your head, keep one arm at your side and extend your other arm straight above your head in the water to touch the wall. Be sure to look for the far wall corner.

Ch. 9 Elementary backstroke progression

48. GENERAL IDEA DEMONSTRATION OF THE ELEMENTARY BACKSTROKE

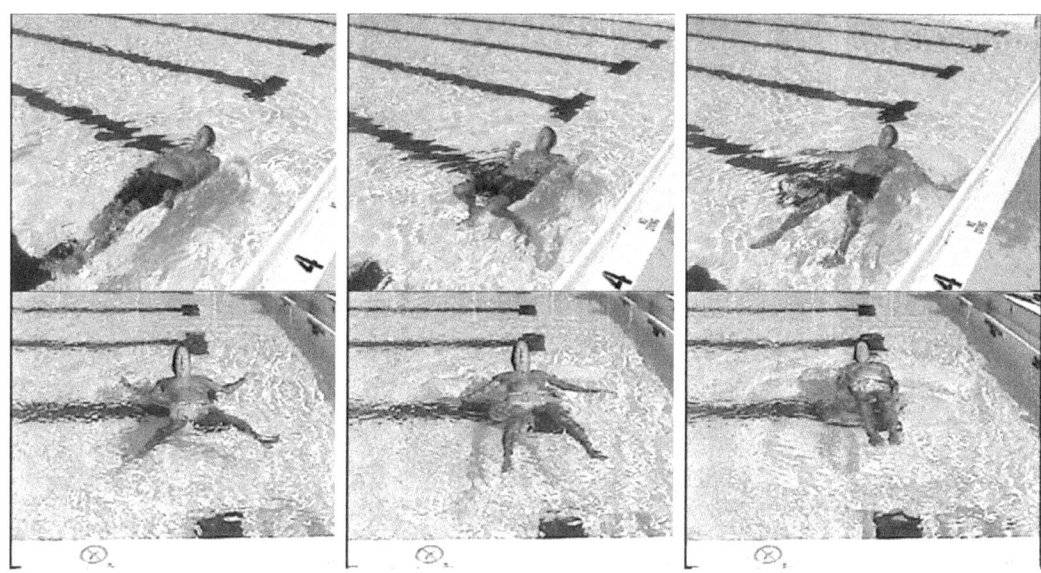

Elementary backstroke is not a competitive swimming stroke. But by learning how to do this stroke, you can observe your breaststroke kick on your back to gain valuable feedback to do it correctly. This is a resting stroke that uses up less air and energy to go farther distances. Its only drawback occurs when waves crash over your face, up your nose, and into your mouth which may cause you to choke and panic.

Your arms and legs provide propulsion at the same time, and then go into a real long glide for as much as 6'. Your hands slide up along your sides as opposed to recovering over-the-top like regular backstroke. Then you rotate your arms and hands directly outward from your armpits to press sideways back to your sides in a long resting glide. Your kick will have three separate subroutines which I will teach you to help master the breaststroke kick very quickly kicking on your back.

49. REVIEW THE BACK FLOAT NEUTRAL POSITION

Your streamlined body position in the back float happens when you bring your shoulder blades back together, get your ears wet, and place your focus on the right cues. You can slightly scull your hands keeping your arms at your sides to boost up your hips and keep your torso level without sitting down. If your legs start to drop, do a moderate flutter kick to stay level. In this correct body position, you can feel good forward movement when you finish your arms and legs for the elementary backstroke propulsion.

50. REVIEW SCULLING TO FEEL THE WATER PRESSURE

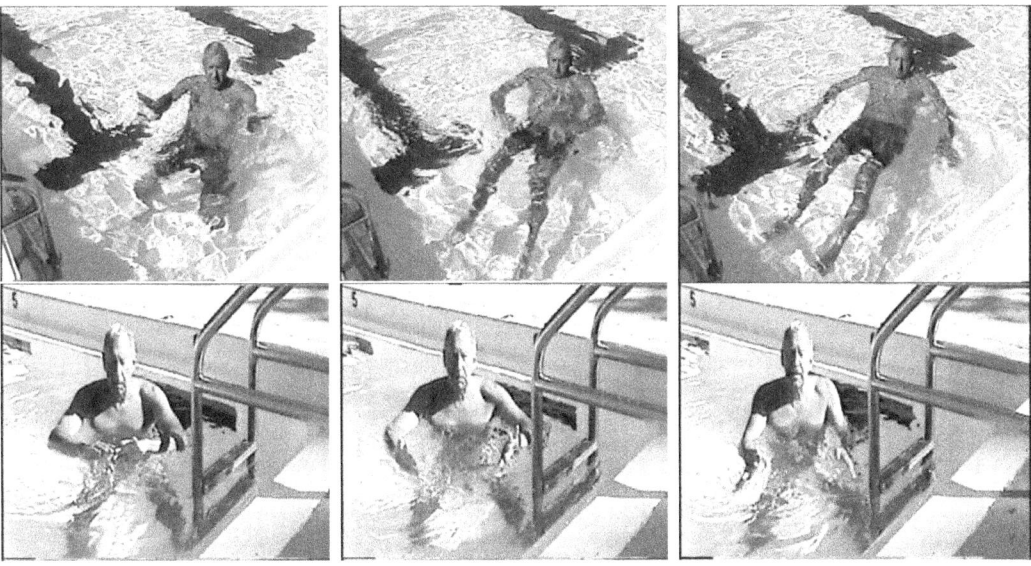

Your palms are flat as if you were spreading sand out on a table top or waving and making a figure 8. Feel the water pressure continuously on your palms rotating around your wrist. Sculling assists in keeping your hips up so that you can look back at your legs to see your breaststroke kick. Be sure to master sculling.

51. CHAIN SUB ROUTINES OR PARTS OF A SKILL TOGETHER

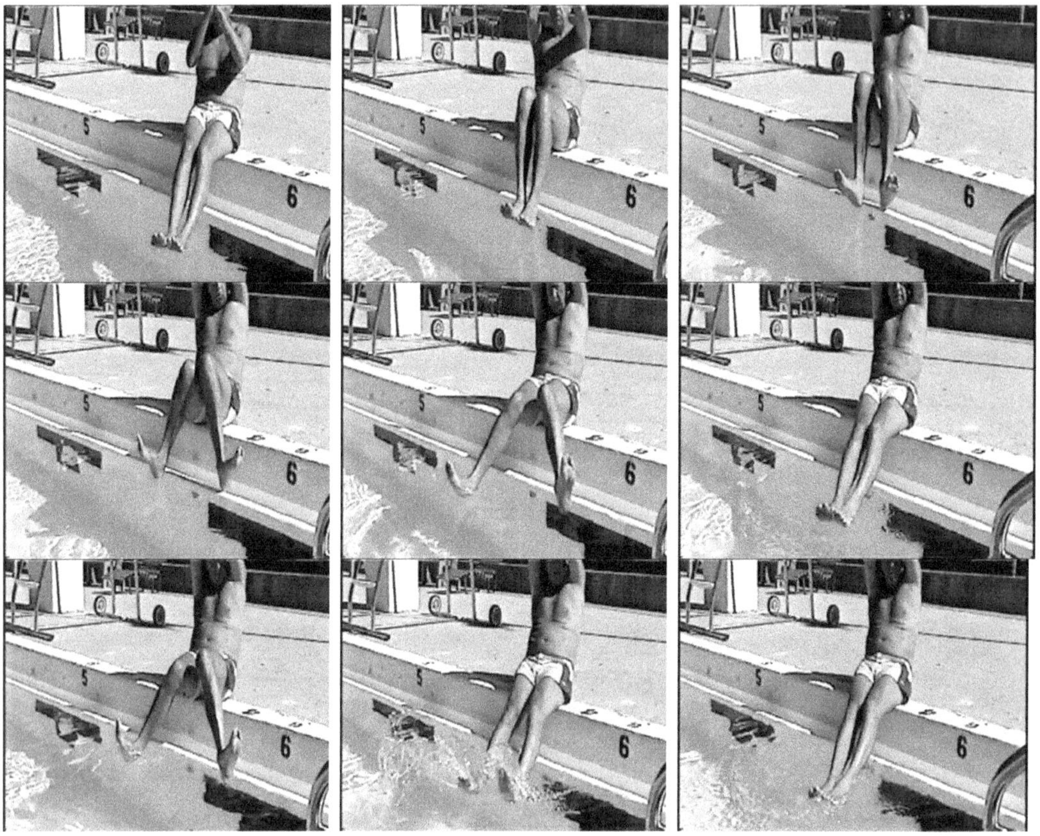

I break down the whole breaststroke kick into three separate parts that you can easily master one at a time. Once you master each, I chain the parts in sequence back together in one continuous motion. This helps you learn this kick faster and build your confidence.

52. FOOT SHAPE PHYSICS - BERNOULLI'S PRINCIPLE APPLIED TO BREASTSTROKE KICKING

Take a look at your foot. The inside border is thicker than the outside border. Shaped like an airplane wing to get lift and fly, your foot slides through the water at an angle in a circular motion. This laminar flow creates pressure gradient differences that cause molecules of water to rapidly form underneath the bottom of your foot just as air molecules form underneath an airplane wing to give it lift. When you get pressure under your feet and kick directly backward with your foot in a circular motion, your body can go directly forward.

Ch. 10 Elementary backstroke kick sub routines pairing up visual, verbal, and kinesthetic (feeling) cues

53. MAKE A "V" WITH YOUR FEET LIKE SEAL FLIPPERS

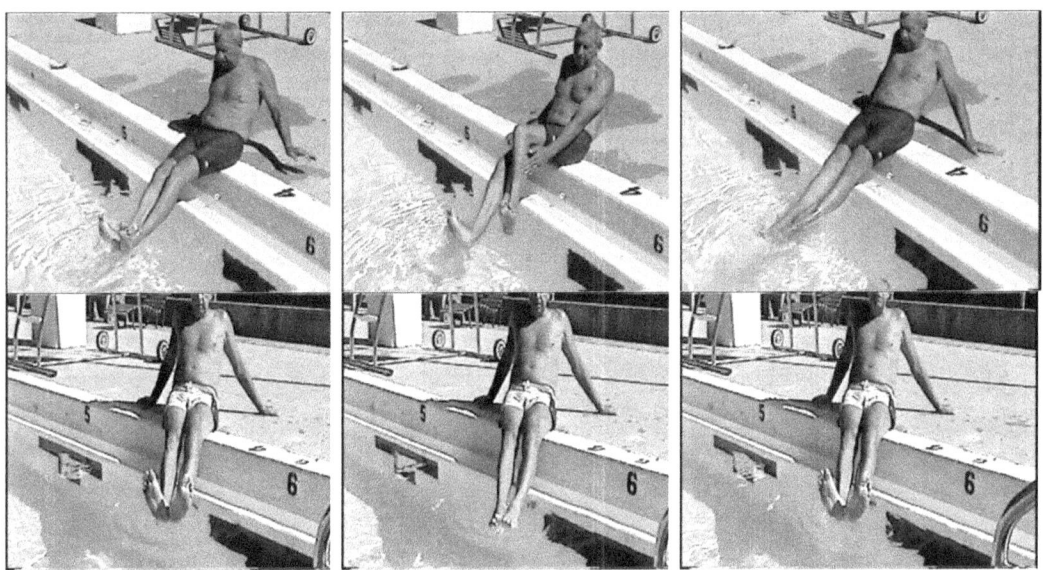

Sit on the pool edge, a chair or bench, and lean back with your legs together. Point your toes, and flex your ankles to make a "V" with your feet. Your heels touch at the "V" bottom. To condition this ankle flexion sub routine, go from a toe point to the "V" and return 4-5 times. On the last flexion hold the "V" until you feel the muscle tension on the outside of your lower leg start to get tired. This is an important kinesthetic feeling cue. When you are on your stomach in the water and unable to see your feet, you will know by feel if you're in the correct position for each ankle by how your muscle feels in your lower leg.

54. DO A LEG DRIVE WITH YOUR LEGS TOGETHER UP AND BACK LIKE A PISTON WITH YOUR FEET IN THE "V"

This is the dominant action of your kick. When kids jump up in basketball, they do not start with their legs spread way apart. Their feet are directly under their hips to drive downward to go upward. In this kick, you have the same dominant action to bring your legs up, and shoot them back hard to get maximum propulsion to go forward.

Don't rotate your heels out yet. You only want to condition this dominate motor pattern first. It serves no purpose to shoot your legs outward outside of the midline and create excessive resistance to your forward movement. The inner border of your foot will not slide through the water to create lift under the bottom of your foot to propel you forward.

Bring your knees and heels up equally outside the midline like you would squat down and keep your balance. To bring either your knees or heels up more creates too much resistance. Keep your heels just below the surface of the water. As you draw your legs up, form the "V" flexing your ankles so that your toes point up towards your kneecaps. Keep your legs together and your feet flexed up in the "V". Then do 4-5 up and back motions pausing at the end of your thrust back each time to condition this piston-like leg drive action.

55. SPREAD YOUR HEELS TO ROTATE APART AND BACK TOGETHER AGAIN FROM YOUR LOWER LEG KEEPING YOUR KNEES UP TOGETHER AND FEET IN THE "V"

  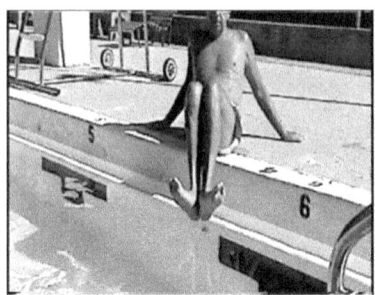

With your legs up, feet in the "V" and your toes pointing up towards your kneecaps, spread only your heels 12-18 inches apart and back together again. Condition this lower leg rotation out and back from your knee. In technical terms, this is medial rotation of your femur.

Do this 5-6 times pausing when your heels are fully rotated apart. You will start to feel muscle tension in your hip rotator muscles to know you are doing it correctly. Condition this feeling to know it when you are floating and cannot observe your legs and feet before you fire your kick backward in the piston action.

56. CHAINING THE THREE SUB ROUTINES TOGETHER IN THE NEUTRAL FACE FLOAT POSITION

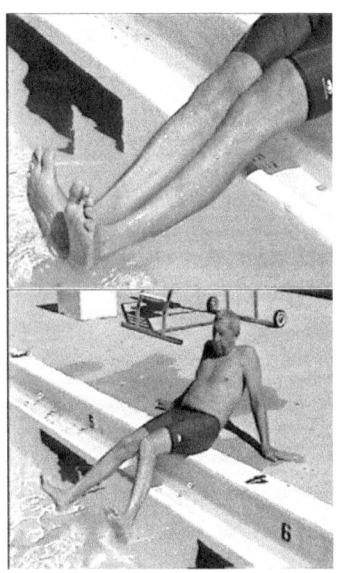  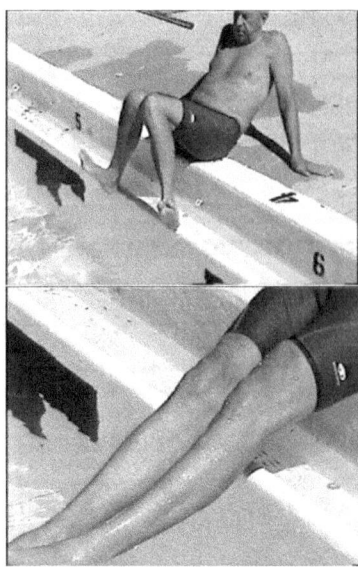

Sit and lean back on the pool edge. In sequence, make your "V" and bring your legs up. Do your spread and hold. Make a mental movie of your entire pattern and remember how your muscles feel as you do each sub routine in the sequence. When you kick, drive your heels straight back like in the piston step. Notice how your legs come together automatically in a face float glide position. For any part of your legs, little time is spent outside of the streamlined midline body position while floating. This reduces resistance and increases your efficiency.

In the old way, people were told to kick their legs wide and squeeze them together. Can you imagine the zero thrust you get from moving two logs together? Or, jumping up with your legs already spread apart? Your foot cannot make a circular motion to get lift and use Bernoulli's Principle.

Later you will transfer these identical elements to do in your face float position in sequence. Your feedback will be to feel the thrust, and see if your body moves forward. If correct, you will move significantly forward to know you can teach yourself.

Ch. 11 Elementary backstroke kicking for power – not a frog, wedge, whip, squeeze, or by any other name but breaststroke

Do all of these in a wall brace with your arms fully extended directly facing the wall; prepare for thrust to protect your teeth from hitting the wall

57. DO 3-5 "V" FLIPPERS WITH YOUR ARMS FULLY EXTENDED IN THE NEUTRAL POSITION ON THE WALL

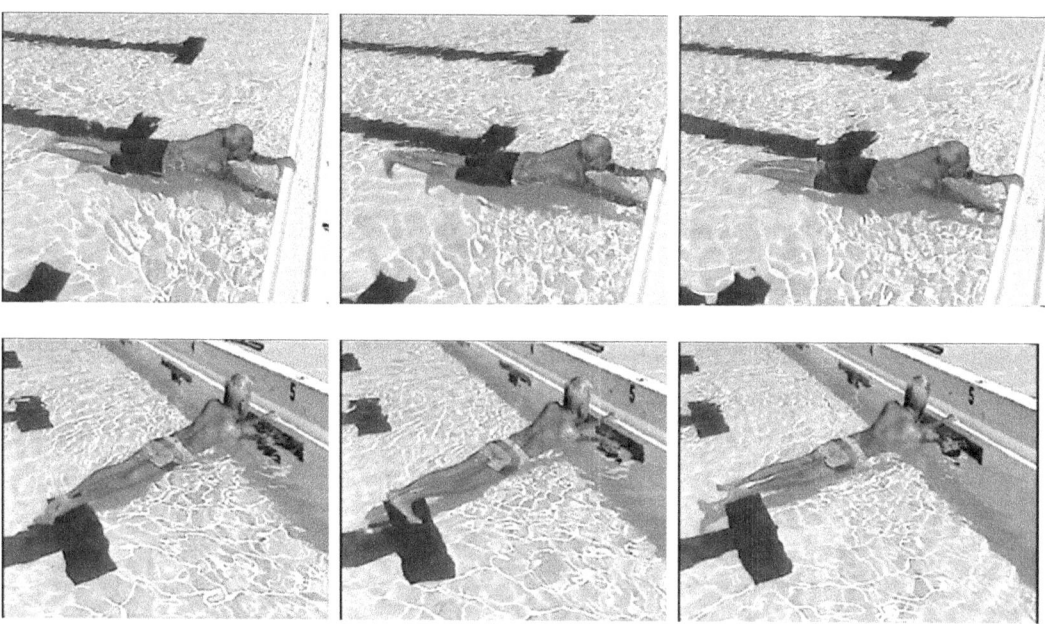

Using the wall brace, exert pressure with your lower hand to hold your legs up in the neutral position. Practice 3-5 ankle flexes up in the "V" feeling the muscle tension on your lower leg as you saw it before on the deck. Point your toes feet together, and then flex your ankles back up so your toes point up towards your kneecaps. Make your toe point (plantar flexion) and ankle flexion (dorsi flexion) multiple times with your eyes closed to feel it, and know you are doing the pattern correctly.

58. MAKE THE "V" AS YOU BRING YOUR LEGS UP AND BACK LIKE A PISTON

Form the "V" as you bring both legs up together like doing a full squat and keeping your balance. Avoid only bringing up your heels, as they will form a brake to create more resistance. Beginners who bring their heels up out of the water also point their toes and forget to flex their ankles to make the "V". Neither should you focus on only bringing your knees up. The piston action is like doing a squat you can do on the deck and stand back up without losing your balance. This keeps your legs closer to the imaginary midline to reduce resistance. Practice moving your legs up and back together in the "V" position until you master this step.

59. MAKE THE "V", BRING YOUR LEGS UP TOGETHER, AND HOLD IN THAT POSITION TO DO THE SPREAD 3-5 TIMES

This step adds on to the two previous steps in the sequence. After your legs are up together and your feet are in the "V", spread apart only your heels while keeping your thighs together. Then move your heels back together and apart to feel the rotation of your lower leg outside of your upper leg or knee. Condition this feeling by spreading apart your heels, and holding them apart for several seconds to feel the muscle tension in your hip rotators.

Later, floating on your stomach, you chain these three sub routines together. With loss of vision, you put your kick into the ready position based on the feeling cues you conditioned from your muscles. Like aiming a gun and getting ready to pull the trigger, use your muscles to feel the tension and position of your feet and legs. When ready, say "kick" to yourself and drive your heels straight back as hard as you would to stomp on a bug or jump up in the air. Your feet will come together automatically into your glide position.

Make sure you stop at the end of each kick. This resets your mental sequence of events to learn the kick.

Ch. 12   Child guidance – breaststroke kicking wall brace position standing one foot behind the end of his/her kick

60. HOLD FLEXED FOOT HEELS UP, AND GUIDE HIS FEET TO MAKE THE "V" PATTERN

Cradle the bottom of his foot in your hand to rotate his toes outward to make the "V" and feel him flexing his ankles up. If he is not thinking about the action, you can easily un-flex his ankles. Then point his toes up toward his knees making the "V". At the same time, have him flex his ankles up to make the "V" while you provide slight resistance for him to feel the muscle flexion needed. Keep repeating this action until you feel he has conditioned how to feel the muscle tension in his lower leg to know he is doing the ankle flexion correctly and holding it.

Test his muscle tension to maintain his ankle flexion up by lightly trying to move his feet into a toe point. He must overcome your resistance. Do this pattern correctly 3-5 times.

61. HOLD FLEXED FOOT HEELS UP, FORM THE "V", AND DO 3-5 LEGS UP AND BACK TOGETHER

Stand with your one foot forward far enough behind your child so you are not kicked. Grasp his feet to do the piston action up and back. Insist that he keep his legs together the whole time while keeping his feet in the "V" position. If you feel his ankle relax in the "V" and not fully flex up, remind him to feel the muscle tension in his lower leg when he flexes his ankles up. He must do 3-5 up and back piston action patterns correctly with a slight stop at the end of each kick. You will guide his feet through the entire pattern slowly and with slight resistance.

NOTE: Be careful to tell him not to thrust off your hands or he will shoot his face into the wall. He must keep his arms fully extended and braced for any kind of thrust he may feel. After mastery of the pattern, you can have him float and thrust off your hands in the open water.

62. HOLD FLEXED FOOT HEELS UP, FORM THE "V", AND BRING THE LEGS UP TOGETHER AND HOLD TO DO 3-5 SPREAD ROUTINES

In the legs up "V" position, rotate his lower leg outside the upper leg to spread the heels apart and back together again. Do 4-5 times keeping his feet in the water pausing at the end of the rotation to condition the feeling in his hip muscles. Have him focus on keeping his ankles flexed up when he does the spread. Otherwise, one foot will relax and end up doing a scissors kick and achieve no propulsion.

63. CHAIN THE BREASTSTROKE KICK PARTS TOGETHER IN SLOW PATTERN MOVEMENT PROVIDING FOOT RESISTANCE TO FEEL WHAT THE WATER PRESSURE WILL BE LIKE

His arms are fully extended away from the wall. Do a slow pattern movement to simulate water resistance, but do not apply too much resistance during the pattern or he will push off your hands and drive his face into the wall. You only want him to feel the sequence of the three sub routines being chained together to do the entire pattern. At the end of each sub routine, stop to emphasize his focus on the muscle feel that he cannot see. Then when you have him float, he can copy that same feeling before he kicks back.

Ch. 13 Elementary backstroke kicking on your back transfer identical kick elements from dry land and wall brace sub routines to see in your back float

64. REVIEW SCULLING MOTION TO ASSIST YOUR BACK FLOAT TO LOOK AT YOUR BREASTSTROKE LEG PATTERN AND GAIN FEEDBACK

 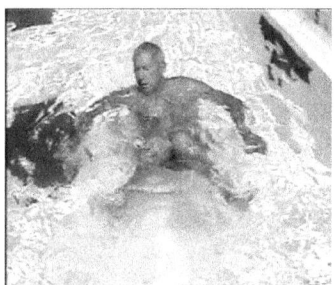 

Scull to keep your body somewhat level to look at your legs doing each of the three sub routines. Then do each again in sequence. Focus on what you see and feel at the same time to self-correct each sub routine. Do a back glide and scull 10-20 feet and look at your legs and feet doing each sub routine to gain feedback from your kick movement.

65. PUSH OFF THE WALL, BACK GLIDE WITH YOUR SCULLING ASSIST

Continue to practice your back glide with your sculling to feel more comfortable getting ready to view your breaststroke kick on your back. You will sit out slightly as you draw your legs up. Don't worry about keeping your body position, but try to keep your back level as your head looks back to see your legs and feet practice the patterns of each sub routine. Your sculling will keep you from sitting up completely.

66. IN YOUR BACK GLIDE POSITION MAKE A "V" AND HOLD FOR 5 SECONDS TO FEEL THE MUSCLE TENSION

Scull to keep your back float and look at your feet making a "V". Feel the muscle tension in your lower leg when you hold that position. Now flipper your feet to the toe point and ankle flex back into the "V" several times to condition this sub routine while floating and sculling.

67. IN YOUR BACK GLIDE POSITION WITH THE "V", BRING YOUR LEGS UP AND BACK TOGETHER LIKE A PISTON

See your legs come up and back together like a piston while forming and keeping the "V" with your feet as you thrust back. This action is also like stomping on a bug. You would break your foot if you pointed your toes doing that. Pretend the bug is crawling on an imaginary wall behind you. If you still don't get it, then get out of the pool and practice this action on one foot on the deck.

Try to hold in that position for several seconds doing your sculling if necessary. Now kick directly backward like a piston keeping your feet in the "V" and your legs together. Repeat this action several times to condition the pattern. Focus on stopping at the end of your kick for at least 2 seconds. You can count to yourself 1, 2. This timing will let you do your arms while your kick is still streamlined.

68. IN YOUR BACK GLIDE POSITION FORM THE "V" AND BRING YOUR LEGS UP TOGETHER; THEN SPREAD YOUR HEELS APART AND BACK TOGETHER 3-5 TIMES

Bring your legs up together forming and keeping your ankles flexed up in the "V" first. Then spread only your heels apart and back together several times keeping your upper legs together. On the last one, spread apart and hold for 3-4 seconds to feel and condition the muscle tension in your hip while floating on your back. That pause will help you get into that position when you turn over in your face float to learn to kick breaststroke on your stomach. The feeling helps you to know you are in position when you can no longer see your legs and feet.

69. CHAIN TOGETHER THE KICK PARTS OR SUB ROUTINES IN SEQUENCE STOPPING TO HOLD IN EACH POSITION, THEN KICK BACK HARD FROM THE SPREAD INTO A LONG GLIDE

Focus on seeing and feeling to do each part separately. It will appear jerky as you pause to assume each position in the sequence - "V", legs up, spread - kick and glide. Scull to keep your hips up and maintain your body position so that you don't sit down. A correct kick makes you glide 3-4 feet for your positive feedback.

70. BACK PUSH OFF AND GLIDE, THEN ADD ONLY 2-3 KICKS WITH A GLIDE STOP FOR 3 SECONDS EACH TIME

From your push off and glide do some sculling, and watch your feet and legs go through the entire kick pattern step-by-step in the sequence. Eventually it will look like one continuous motion. Focus on stopping and gliding at the end of every kick. This creates the timing for your pull to do its part. If you don't stop and draw your legs up too soon, you work against yourself trying to do your pull and kick at the same time creating too much resistance. Note that when your feet kick directly backward from the spread position your legs come together automatically streamlined. This reduces resistance to be more efficient.

The painted lane lines indicate how far you go with each kick. This feedback indicates your efficiency to teach yourself.

Ch. 14 Elementary Backstroke Arm Progression

71. DEMONSTRATION OF FULL ARM PATTERN AND GLIDE STOP - FEELS LIKE YOUR FOLLOW-THROUGH IN THE BACKSTROKE

Your arms recover up under the water next to your side at the same time. When your hands reach up under your armpits, they extend directly outward. Rotate your forearms sideways, and start to press backward. The end of your arm pull press is like the follow-through in regular backstroke except that your shoulders do not rotate and remain level. Be sure to stop and glide on your back at the end of each stroke to increase your distance per stroke for more efficiency. This is a relaxing stroke that helps you recover your breath if you ever get into trouble.

72. START YOUR ARMS SEQUENCE WITH YOUR RECOVERY AND THEN GO INTO YOUR CATCH, ROTATION, AND FOLLOW-THROUGH INTO A LONG BACK GLIDE

From your back float position, practice drawing your hands up together along your sides up to your armpits. Then using your lower arms, rotate your hand and forearm directly outward and sideways to feel the water pressure as you draw your elbows into your body to make your press backward. Slightly accelerate the press in your stroke, and try to keep excellent body position to reduce resistance.

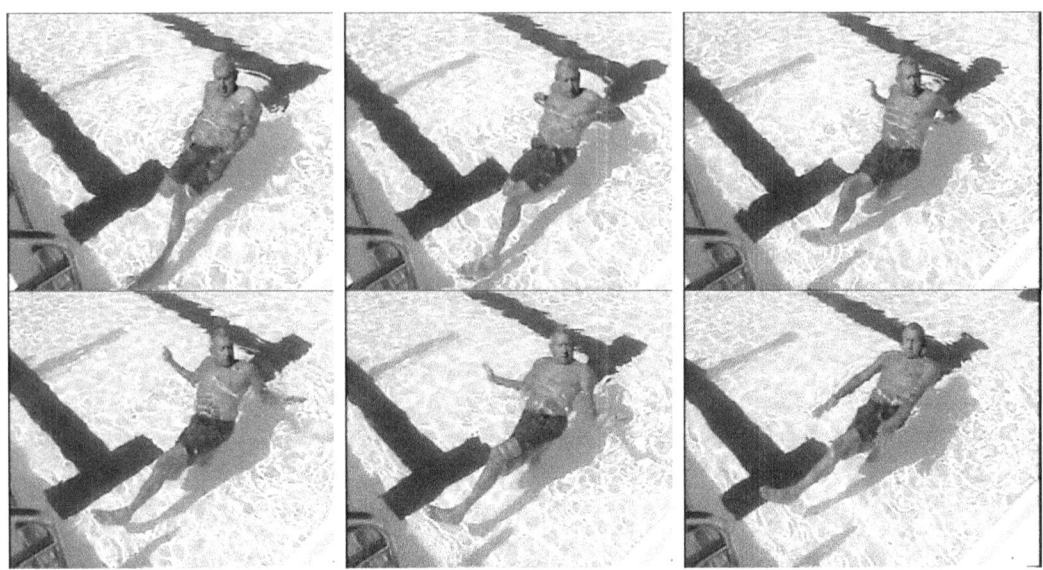

73. PUSH OFF THE WALL INTO YOUR BACK GLIDE AND DO 2-3 PULLS ONLY WITH A GLIDE STOP AT THE END OF YOUR PULL FOR 2-3 SECONDS EACH TIME

Remember you are floating. Scull to assist keeping your body position. Do only 2-3 arm pulls, and glide 2-3 seconds at the end of each pull. To reduce resistance on your recovery, slowly draw your hands up along your sides to your armpits. Emphasize the power in your arm pulls to give yourself a longer press in your follow through to glide farther. The glide will give you time to rest and not burn up all your energy. Notice how many lines you cross increases as you improve your streamlining and body position.

Ch. 15 Elementary backstroke timing your arms and legs – stand on the pool deck or in the shallow end

74. SEWING MACHING – IMAGINE A STRING ATTACHED FROM YOUR ELBOWS TO YOUR KNEES

Visualize a string between your elbows and your knees. As you recover your arms up along your sides, your knees will be pulled up by your elbows attached to that string. As you press your arms backward, you will also be kicking into your long glide. Your elbows or knees will not travel up very much to reduce resistance.

75. ARMS AND LEGS – START BOTH UP AND BACK AT THE SAME TIME

Practice timing the recovery of your arms and your legs to start each stroke at the same time. In your back glide or float think about the start. Do 4-5 times to feel the pattern start from your glide. You don't need to do the entire stroke, but work on the recovery timing of your arms and legs.

76. PUSH OFF THE WALL INTO YOUR GLIDE AND ADD THE RECOVERY OF YOUR ARMS AND LEGS, THEN PULL AND KICK BACKWARD AT THE SAME TIME TO DO 2-3 GOOD STROKES WITH LONG GLIDES

After you condition each subroutine, it's time to put them all together in the sequence. Push off to start a good back float. Then start to recover your hands, arms, and legs up into position to pull and kick at the same time into a long glide. Practice doing several strokes one at a time with long glides.

77. DO 2-3 STROKES WITH LONG GLIDES ACROSS THE POOL IN THE SHALLOW END

Focus on your body position to gain feedback for how far you will go with each stroke in your glide. Longer glides mean more efficiency. Feel the water pressure on your hands and forearms to accelerate in the follow-through. Your knees may come out of the water surface a little. Focus on spreading your heels apart wider than your knees. Keep your upper legs together. Feel the thrust of your legs going back together from the spread position maintaining the "V" as long as you can. Your toes will point automatically in your glide; don't think about that.

Ch. 16 Water safety proof - teach your children to prove their skills; share your videos and save more lives

78. PROVE YOUR SKILLS

Boys 14 and under account for 80% of the unintentional drowning deaths because they overestimate their swimming ability. No matter what age or ability, if you are as good as you say or think you are, then demonstrate each of these curriculum steps in a minimal amount of time. If you cannot demonstrate a step, go back and master the previous step. Keep going back until you can demonstrate your mastery to yourself.

You may think you learned how to swim correctly, but there are gaps in your learning. Reading this book and watching my video series will help you. If you are a competitor, you cannot improve your times until you improve your efficient skills. Every record holder I know is constantly looking to improve his or her technique, and so can you.

79. DON'T SAY YOU CAN UNTIL YOU CAN PROVE IT BY SHOWING YOUR SKILLS IN EACH STEP

Don't let your children or grandchildren tell you they can do any step until they can show you and apply this same message to your own skills. As you learn how to perform each skill share your knowledge with others. The greatest gift you can give someone is to overcome their swimming fears.

I constantly preach, "You float first, and swim second." When you are comfortable floating, your brain can process sensory information more clearly to improve your focus on specific skills.

To compete and swim farther faster, you must overcome resistance with good technique, and increase your strength to accelerate your propulsion force. Knowing how without practice will not help. You must condition the feeling cues to gain spatial awareness of your body position at all times to get streamlined.

80. GOOD SAFE SWIMMING IS <u>NOT</u> WITH YOUR HEAD COMPLETELY OUT OF WATER

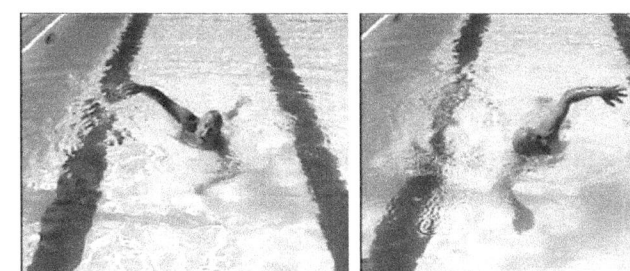

When your head is up out of the water, your hips and legs must go down. Would you rather be a water ski or a barge? To keep your head out of water while swimming, you must push down more than push back to get forward momentum. You will tire out very quickly and get in trouble. You need to know how to swim continuously by exchanging a small portion of your air supply with each complete right or left arm (as you may choose) breathing stroke.

Do not assume drowning will happen to the other guy or their family. The life you save may be your own if you take action now to keep improving your skills and knowledge. It only takes a few minutes to get into trouble. Knowledge of your swimming skills and abilities, and the power of water can prevent an accident. By investing in this book and videos, you have taken action to follow the wisdom that, "an ounce of prevention, is worth a pound of cure."

81. LEARN HOW TO SWIM WITH PROPER BREATHING

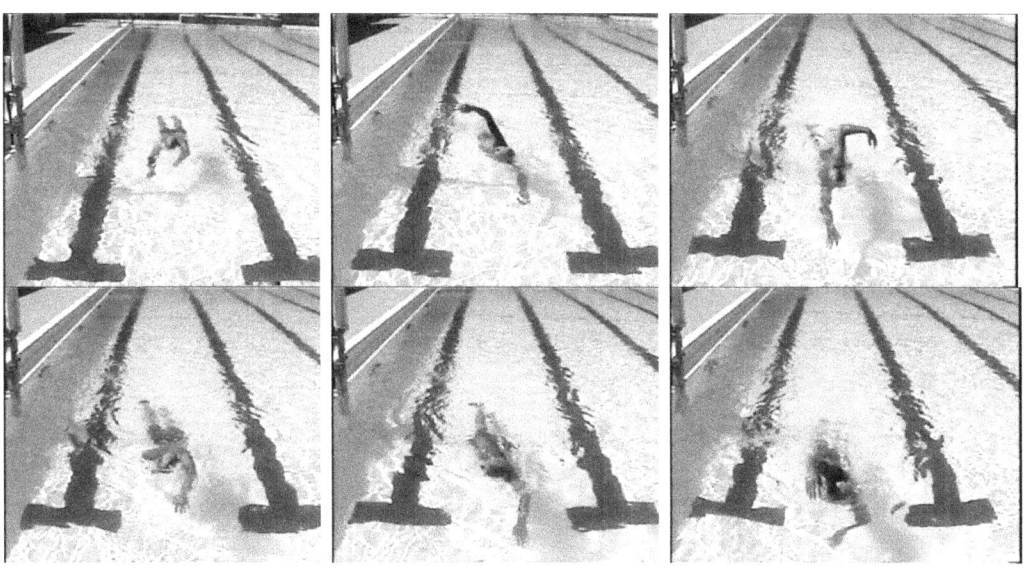

(This is a summary reminder from earlier chapters). Imagine that rod or spindle running through your body from the top of your head to your feet to keep your alignment or body position. You rotate or roll your shoulders and body around that rod. You avoid side to side or up and down movements outside of that imaginary midline to improve your streamlining technique. Use the feeling or kinesthetic cues I taught you to get more spatial awareness of your body parts, know if you are streamlined, and lengthen your stroke.

Use the phrase I taught you earlier to "pull, take a breath, put your head back down, and bring your other arm around." These words trigger your body parts to get into a consistent rhythm to breathe every stroke starting to exhale as soon as your face goes back down after inhaling. If you take short strokes or swim too hard by being inefficient, you build up an oxygen debt you are not able to replace and have to stop. This may be okay in a swimming pool, but not in a lake or the ocean where you cannot see or touch bottom. Yes you can float or tread water to get some of your air back and recover, but you still have made no forward progress toward safety.

Why quit swimming lessons if you only know how to swim a short distance without mastery of your breathing? Adults frequently get into trouble thinking they are 12 years old, and can stop and rest at any time. You are never too old to teach yourself how to master this skill after you easily master floating.

82. SHARE YOUR BOOK AND VIDEOS; SAVE MORE LIVES

The mission of this book and video series is to save more lives. These resources benefit no one collecting dust on your shelf. They are an investment that can be shared with all your family, relatives, friends, co-workers, and neighbors. Get your local community and high school libraries to invest in a copy. Share this valuable resource, and your knowledge to provide tips to others. Just as easily as you have taught yourself each step to master a variety of skills in this series, you can also teach others what you have done step-by-step in the sequence. Who knows if that one tip you provide may save someone's life?

83. A CLEAR POOL IS NOT LIKE OTHER PLACES

A practical problem exists when you swim in any other aquatic environment. You get used to a clear heated pool, and then find yourself in a flood or muddy lake where you cannot see the bottom. The water may be cold. The first time I swam in a quarry I could not see the bottom clearly, but there seemed to be large scary objects down there. In any unfamiliar environment, lack of local knowledge is dangerous. You have to know the power of water in waves, and flowing rivers. You also have to be aware of varieties of marine life, bacteria, and parasites.

If your floating skills are not good, you are taking a high risk to enter the water. Some fears are unfounded facts. There are people who scuba dive multiple times and have never seen a shark - ever! Anytime you enter an unfamiliar environment and do not know what to expect, you are more likely to tense up your muscles and panic. It's mandatory that you understand water safety concerns beyond your local pool to protect yourself and your family.

My final advice is that you never overestimate your swimming ability. Be familiar with your environment before you venture in the water.

Ask yourself, "How soon could an emergency vehicle reach me?"

"Is there a lifeguard on duty? Is my swim buddy capable?"

Would you ever advise a stranger of the dangers swimming in some unfamiliar places?

Remember skills without knowledge can be dangerous. So please share what you have learned on your social media pages to help save more lives!

If you like this book, write a positive review on Amazon and tell your friends about it on social media to help save more lives.

Here is a link to find this book linked to your Amazon review:

http://www.LearnToSwimProgram.com/Amazon-Reviews